ENGAGING THE COURTS

for

OWNERSHIP & ORDER

Receiving Release from False Claims of Ownership & Resetting Your Life

by

Dr. Ron M. Horner

ENGAGING THE COURTS

for

OWNERSHIP & ORDER

Receiving Release from False Claims of Ownership & Resetting Your Life

by

Dr. Ron M. Horner

LifeSpring Books
PO Box 2167
Albemarle, NC 28002

www.courtsofheavenbook.com

Engaging the Courts for Ownership & Order

Copyright © 2018 Dr. Ron M. Horner

Unless marked otherwise, Scripture is taken from the New King James Version®. Copyright © 1982 by Thomas Nelson. Used by permission. All rights reserved. (Unless otherwise noted.)

Scripture quotations marked (AMP) are taken from the Amplified® Bible (AMP), Copyright © 1954, 1958, 1962, 1964, 1965, 1987 by The Lockman Foundation.

Scripture quotations marked (ASV) are from the American Standard Bible (1901) Public Domain

All rights reserved. This book is protected by the copyright laws of the United States of America. This book may not be copied or reprinted for commercial gain or profit. The use of short quotations or occasional page copying for personal or group study is permitted and encouraged. Permission will be granted upon request.

Requests for bulk sales discounts, editorial permissions, or other information should be addressed to:

LifeSpring Books
PO Box 2167
Albemarle, NC 28002 USA

Additional copies available at www.courtsofheavenbook.com

ISBN 13 Paperback: 978-0-359-07947-6
ISBN 13 eBook: 978-0-359-07945-2

Cover Design by Darian Horner Design (www.darianhorner.com)

Cover Images © AdobeStock #74063608, #202697770, #73285755

10 9 8 7 6 5 4 3 2

Printed in the United States of America

Contents

Acknowledgments I
Foreword III
Preface VII
Chapter 1 Upsetting the Apple Cart 1
Chapter 2 Emotional Liens 21
Chapter 3 Ties That Bind 25
Chapter 4 Bondage of a Religious Flavor 35
Chapter 5 Medical Diagnoses 41
Chapter 6 Modern Day Slavery 45
Chapter 7 The Court of Titles and Deeds 51
Chapter 8 QuickGuide-Court of Titles & Deeds . 61
Chapter 9 Correcting Time 69
Chapter 10 What Do I Do Next? 79
Chapter 11 Accessing the Realms of Heaven 85
Chapter 12 The Court of Records 91
Chapter 13 The Court of Angels 95
Chapter 14 Entire QuickGuide-Personal 99
Chapter 15 Entire QuickGuidefor Others 111
Chapter 16 Conclusion 123

Bibliography 127
Description 129
About the Author 131
Recommended Resources................................ 133

Acknowledgments

As I finish writing this book, it is my mothers' 85th birthday so I want to acknowledge her love and support throughout my life. To my friends Becky, Katherine, Jackie, Michael, Judy, and others who directly supported me in this effort, thank you. Thank you, Tracy for introducing me to the Court of Titles and Deeds and thank you Pamela G. for expanding the possibilities within this court to me and so many others. Blessings to you all!

And, as always thank you Adina, my beautiful wife.

Foreword

Just a few weeks ago (late August of 2018), I was introduced, by Pamela Grisham, to a couple of books. They were written by a person that I had briefly met at a meeting in Oklahoma the previous year. Both of them were on the subject – The Courts of Heaven. My first inclination was not to read them, but to thank her for sharing them with me. She offered to let me borrow her copies, but I declined – partially because I like to purchase my own copies so that I can make my own notations in the book, but also because I wasn't sure yet about the author and the book's contents.

I had first heard about, and fully embraced, the revelation regarding the Courts of Heaven a few years ago as it was taught by my friend Robert Henderson. Since then I have passed on the teaching to others and have taught it myself on many occasions. Let me state here a common issue in my life that has raised its ugly head on occasion. In my mind I would declare, "I know about this subject" or "I've read about this before." And as in every previous occasion, the Lord reprimanded me.

On the day of Sunday worship when Pamela first shared the books, I had not even made it home before the Lord prompted me to order them. The two books, *The Courts of Heaven: An Introduction* (now known as *Engaging the Mercy Court of Heaven*) and the second book *Overcoming Verdicts from the Courts of Hell: Releasing False Judgments* arrived a couple of days later. I picked up the first one and began to read it. I did not set it down until I was finished a couple of hours later. I was overwhelmed. The other book was on Kindle and so I started it as well. Same story – same outcome.

Both books brought a fresh, powerful and practical (hands on) approach to the topic. I have told people that "life is a beach" as long as it's a beach on a lake. I love the ocean and sound of the roaring breakers, but if I have a choice, I would rather sit by a lake and meditate on its beauty. That is the power of Dr. Ron Horner's books. When he sent me the manuscript for *Engaging the Courts for Ownership and Order*, and asked me to do the foreword, I was honored. With the same experience, I devoured it on my flight to Washington D.C. Interestingly, I was going to our nation's capital to pray on-site at the Judge Kavanaugh Supreme Court Hearings. The book came alive in my spirit as I sat there interceding before the

Supreme Court of Heaven on behalf of Judge Kavanaugh.

As a final word, do not read this book or his other books in order to just gain more information. Do what is written in this book! It is a practical guide which will help throw off the shackles of the enemy and unlock the true destiny that you possess as His child. Acknowledge the access that has been granted to us as sons and daughters of the King and "approach with confidence" the court of our Supreme Judge.

Dr. Thomas Schlueter
Texas Apostolic Prayer Network
Prince of Peace House of Prayer
Arlington, Texas

Preface

It was a Thursday morning in late summer when the download from Heaven came. Only four days before my understanding of the Court of Titles and Deeds had been expanded to consider the ownership of people as a real problem with far-reaching consequences. I was aware of sex-trafficking and other slavery issues but had not put all the pieces together.

On this particular morning as I sat before the Lord I began to see and hear so much more than I ever imagined. At 8:00 that morning I had an advocacy session in court with a client to deal with a handful of issues that had plagued her family for decades. As we inquired of the Court concerning any outstanding liens or false titles, answers came. With each response, we would handle each situation and move to the next one. One by one, the challenges to ownership were satisfied. The rush of peace was palpable with each issue being dealt with in the Courts.

By the end of our session, freedom had been brought to a number of people and situations – even to their business where the enemy had laid claim to it years before.

Revelation always brings revolution.

The revelation of how to apply this concept had exploded within me. This is what Lynn had to say following that morning session:

Ron, for the first time in years I have excitement in my heart. No anxiousness! Is this how normal people feel? It is beautiful! The peace! Thank you, Lord!

Later that day, with the assistance of my friend Katherine, we accessed the Court of Records where I downloaded the contents of this book to my spirit. Then I began to transcribe what I received which you will read in the pages of this book. May amazing levels of freedom be brought to your life through these fresh understandings of the Courts of Heaven.

-*Ron Horner*

Chapter 1
Upsetting the Apple Cart

The phone call was totally unexpected. Jean an intermediary for a troubled young woman (whom we will call Debbie) and Carol, a Christian counselor answered only to hear someone speaking with fury in their voice. They were incredibly angry that Carol had been to the Courts of Heaven and received a Permanent Restraining Order against them. They threatened to come to her home in person to kill her since they could no longer astral project themselves from place to place. They had been grounded by an order from the Courts of Heaven.

Just prior to this court work, Debbie's owners declared they owned her and astrally projected to her where they repeatedly raped her. They did not want to lose their prized possession.

Debbie's Story

The torment was incredible. For years she had suffered physically and emotionally at the hands of her handlers and owners. She was no more than a piece of property to be used as they deemed fit. If they wanted sex – she delivered. Anything they demanded – she was forced to perform. The price that had been paid for her was immense – a half million dollars. Having been abused since conception, she had suffered a lifetime of unimaginable horror.

Many reading this may find it hard to believe that someone had been bought like cattle at an auction, but it is true. Multiplied thousands have been traded like livestock. This trade is a far more serious dilemma than most people realize.

Her situation seemed so surreal, yet, it was true. She had been living this nightmare for years. Now her cry was for freedom. As she disclosed these things to Carol, she realized she had found the right person to talk to – one who could truly help her find freedom. She found hope again.

Carol, who only a few months before had discovered the Courts of Heaven prayer paradigm, opted to engage the Courts of Heaven with a close friend assisting her on behalf of Debbie. Since Debbie was considered "property" of another person, a venture into the ①Court of Titles and Deeds was the first stop in Debbie's journey to freedom.

They entered this court requesting a Transfer of Title Deed (a transfer of ownership) from the present "owner" and the other parties involved) unto Jehovah God. After a few moments, the Transfer of Title was complete; the foray into the Courts of Heaven was not yet over though. They still had a few stops to make.

The next stop was the ②Court of Records (Scribes) to record the transfer of ownership, and then to the ③Criminal Court to obtain a Permanent Restraining Order against her owners and a number of other pertinent parties. On the scroll pertaining to the restraining order were the instructions that if they violated this Permanent Restraining Order, they would face chains or bondage, imprisonment, or death. This is serious business. One person had already died in a similar scenario by violating one of these orders.

Upon receiving the Permanent Restraining Order, Carol again accessed the ④Court of Records (Scribes) to get these items recorded. While in that court Carol was handed fifteen scrolls related to this situation which they delivered to the Court of Angels for immediate dispatch on behalf of Debbie.

It was apparent that the angels had done their job (and we're continuing to do so) as was evidenced by the phone call they had received. Neither Carol (nor her friend) had told anyone about their visit to the Courts of Heaven, but the demons knew and communicated that information to Debbie's former owners. Their applecart had been upset. Debbie's story is not unlike the owners of the young slave-girl with the spirit of divination recorded in the book of Acts[1]. They could no longer benefit as they had from Debbie.

The final act Carol and her friend took was to receive Communion as a means of sealing what had been done for Debbie. In the intervening time, however, Debbie had been tormented. No more torment occurred after receiving Communion. Oh, the power of the blood and body of Jesus.

In the following days attempts were made by her owners to keep her entrapped, but Carol returned to the Courts of Heaven and obtained a Writ of Assistance to enjoin the angels in formally working to bring Debbie into a full measure of freedom. How many more Debbie's are in the earth is similar straits? May they all find freedom. Also instruction came to extend the restraining order to each personality of the defendant. Often they have dissociative identity

---

[1] Acts 16:16-19

disorder (formerly multiple personality disorder) and each identity needs to be included in the restraining order. In the event of any further violation, the release of High Praises unto God are in order.

> *⁶ Let the high praises of God be in their mouth, and a two-edged sword in their hand, ⁷ To execute vengeance on the nations, and punishments on the peoples; ⁸ to bind their kings with chains, and their nobles with fetters of iron; ⁹ to execute on them the written judgment--this honor have all His saints. Praise the LORD! (Psalm 149:6-9)*

This invites the Lord of Glory into the situation in a powerful way. The Psalmist describes the intervention of the Lord in this way:

> *¹³ The LORD thundered from heaven, and the Most High uttered His voice, hailstones and coals of fire. ¹⁴ He sent out His arrows and scattered the foe, lightnings in abundance, and He vanquished them. ¹⁵ Then the channels of the sea were seen, the foundations of the world were uncovered at Your rebuke, O LORD, at the blast of the breath of Your nostrils. ¹⁶ He sent from above, He took me; He drew me out of many waters. ¹⁷ He delivered me from my strong enemy, from those who hated me, for they were too strong for me. ¹⁸ They confronted*

me in the day of my calamity, but the LORD was my support. [19] He also brought me out into a broad place; He delivered me because He delighted in me. [20] The LORD rewarded me according to my righteousness; according to the cleanness of my hands He has recompensed me. (Psalm 18:13-20)

We have not tapped the power of High Praise in stopping our enemies. We must allow the Lord of Glory to teach us these things.

Who is the Legitimate Owner?

Satan loves to assume things are to his way of thinking whether they are or not. The ownership of Planet Earth is clearly established in Psalm 24, but he failed to get the memo.

The earth is the LORD's, and all its fullness, the world and those who dwell therein. (Psalm 24:1) (ASV)

Many other scriptures attest to the same theme:

"Behold, to the LORD your God belong heaven and the highest heavens, the earth and all that is in it. (Deuteronomy 10:14) (ASV)

The heavens are Yours; the earth also is Yours; the world and all it contains, You have founded them. (Psalm 89:11) (ASV)

He blessed him and said, "Blessed be Abram of God Most High, possessor of heaven and earth. (Genesis 14:19) (ASV)

Now then, if you will indeed obey My voice and keep My covenant, then you shall be My own possession among all the peoples, for all the earth is Mine. (Exodus 19:5) (ASV)

For the earth is the Lord's, and all it contains. (1 Corinthians 10:26) (ASV)

Whatever is under the whole heaven is mine. (Job 41: 11) (ASV)

[10] For every beast of the forest is mine, the cattle on a thousand hills. [11] I know every bird of the mountains, and everything that moves in the field is mine. [12] For the world is mine, and all it contains. (Psalm 50:10-12) (ASV)

"The silver is mine, and the gold is mine," declares the LORD of hosts. (Haggai 2:8) (ASV)

The Lord God is the rightful owner. It was never surrendered at any time to him. We are ALL His possession. God has first claim to all of us. Anyone else has only a secondary and typically false claim. The enemy and people have laid claim and created false title deeds or liens which must be canceled or satisfied. In some cases ownership must be transferred, but in every case, God has provided a solution in the Courts of Heaven.

If you recall the story when Jesus was in the wilderness and being tempted by the devil; Satan makes a proposition to Jesus when he says,

> *⁸ Next, the devil took him to the peak of a very high mountain and showed him all the kingdoms of the world and their glory. ⁹ "I will give it all to you," he said, "if you will kneel down and worship me." ¹⁰ "Get out of here, Satan," Jesus told him. "For the Scriptures say, "You must worship the LORD your God and serve only him." (Matthew 4:8-10)*

Satan had laid claim to the kingdoms of the world. He had essentially placed a lien on it because of the permission granted by Adam and Eve due to their disobedience in the Garden of Eden. They had been assigned as stewards of the garden and failed in their duty, thus surrendering their rights to it. The fact that Jesus did not dispute with Satan in the wilderness about who owned the kingdoms of the world does not mean that what Satan said was necessarily true. It was not the main issue at the time. What was not addressed was the fact that the ownership of the planet and all who dwell upon are the property of the Lord (see the scriptures cited previously). By our disobedience, we can give ourselves over to Satan to do his pleasure, just as we can surrender our lives to God and do his pleasure instead.

Paul pointed out that we have the Holy Spirit who is the guarantee (or down payment) for us:

> [13] *In Him you also trusted, after you heard the word of truth, the gospel of your salvation; in whom also, having believed, you were sealed with the Holy Spirit of promise,* [14] *who is the guarantee of our inheritance until the redemption of the purchased possession, to the praise of His glory. (Ephesians 1:13-14)*

False Title Deeds

When a piece of property is purchased, a Title Deed is issued to the rightful owner. In the event you borrowed money to buy the property, the Title Deed will now involve a lienholder meaning that regardless of any claims that may arise concerning that property the lienholder will be taken care of first. You cannot sell the property to another person and deliver a clean title to the buyer without having first paid any outstanding debt to the lienholder. Once they are paid, a document called "Satisfaction of Lien" is filed stating that they are no longer a lienholder and that the obligations have been satisfied by the owner of the property. The owner then has clear title to the property and can deliver a clean title to the prospective buyer.

Many situations may have caused false titles to be created in our lives. The devil does not mind issuing false verdicts, so why should he mind developing a false title – a counterfeit title and presume ownership of something or someone.

We have all seen situations where the jilted boyfriend or husband, claims ownership of the girlfriend or wife and says, "If I cannot have you, no one can have you!" They have asserted ownership unlawfully. A wife is not "property"...a wife is a helpmate, a partner to help you fulfill the purposes of God. Guys, that girlfriend is NOT your property. She belongs to the Lord. Girls, that boyfriend is NOT *your* property. He also belongs to the Lord. If these types of situations do not cause false titles to be created by Hell, they at least create liens against the person.

Liens

Liens are claims against a particular property. In the American legal system, when you purchase a particular property, and you pay for it in full not having gotten a loan using the property as collateral, you are given a clear or clean title. Many other countries operate in a similar manner.

However, if you got a loan to purchase the property that property became the security for the loan. The lender becomes a lien holder. Whether it was land, a house, a vehicle, or any myriad of other items considered real property, the same situation applies. In order to obtain a clear or clean title, the liens must be satisfied. If you borrowed money to purchase the property, then the money must be repaid (with interest usually) in order for the lienholder to be released from the title.

If you purchased a house having received a loan from the bank, were able to pay off the loan and proof is provided to the court that you had satisfied the terms of the lien, the courts would then issue a document usually called a Satisfaction of Lien on your behalf releasing your property from that lien. Once the obligations of the lien are met, the lienholder no longer has any claim to your property.

Certain things can create a situation where a lien is placed upon us where we no longer have a completely free title to do as we please. These often restrict us from functioning freely. Every sin has a consequence and requires a payment in order for that consequence to be released. The blood of Jesus was the price paid for our sins; however, that blood must be applied to that sin in order for the payment to be enacted and the lien to be satisfied.

> *For even the Son of Man came not to be served but to serve others and to give his life as a ransom for many. (Matthew 20:28) (Italics mine)*

A ransom is a price paid to redeem or repurchase something or someone. Our sins created the need for a ransom to be paid to free us from the bondage created. Jesus Christ, via the shedding of his blood, paid the ultimate price so that I could be free from the unpayable price of sin.

Our sin had essentially sold us into servitude. God saw that and sent a remedy:

> *[19] Don't you realize that your body is the temple of the Holy Spirit, who lives in you and was given to you by God? You do not belong to yourself, [20] for God bought you with a high price. So you must honor God with your body. (1 Corinthians 6:19-20)*

As a believer, God is your rightful owner. The devil, however, wants to assert ownership rights in our lives, and often we give him permission to do so (usually inadvertently). We do not mean to but our actions or words create just such a scenario.

Promissory Notes

Similar to title deed, but simpler in form. It typically is used between family and friends and is less formal (but just as legally binding) as a title deed. It is included in this segment because as we were working in this court for someone, we heard that a note existed that needed to be dissolved.

In the natural arena the note is dissolved via payment in full by the one owing the other party. It can also be cancelled by the one owed at their choosing. In the Courts of Heaven, these notes are satisfied by the ransom paid by Jesus. He applies the payment of His blood to our obligation. In the same manner that a lien becomes a full blown title by fully embracing the concept behind it, so a note can be placed upon someone by engaging in a trade that was not desired by the Lord for that person to make. These trades result in notes that must be dissolved.

For instance, a person desires more influence among a certain group of people. He will surrender something of value to himself - a character trait, integrity, or something else of personal value - in exchange for that influence. Often they will compromise morally, that creates a bondage the enemy will hold over them as a means of extorting them and keeping them from moving forward. Particularly in the arena of moral compromise, unless this note is satisfied, they will never be able to move forward in their walk or purpose to the degree intended by the Lord. Even if they have owned the sin, repented, gone through steps of restoration, and begun moving forward, they are never at the same level as they were prior to the moral failure. The event has ownership of their life. It must be dissolved for them to go forward.

This concept could be extended to other arenas of compromise as well. This is still being explored and future editions may cover the information gleaned as we move forward.

The Story of Naboth's Vineyard

In 1 Kings 21:1-16 we have the story of Ahab and Jezebel and their illegal seizure of Naboth's vineyard. The entire story is important, so it follows:

> [1]*And it came to pass after these things that Naboth the Jezreelite had a vineyard which was in Jezreel, next to the palace of Ahab king of Samaria.* [2] *So Ahab spoke to Naboth, saying, "Give me your vineyard that I may have it for a*

vegetable garden, because it is near, next to my house; and for it I will give you a vineyard better than it. Or, if it seems good to you, I will give you its worth in money." ³ But Naboth said to Ahab, "The LORD forbid that I should give the inheritance of my fathers to you!"

⁴ So Ahab went into his house sullen and displeased because of the word which Naboth the Jezreelite had spoken to him; for he had said, "I will not give you the inheritance of my fathers." And he lay down on his bed, and turned away his face, and would eat no food.

⁵ But Jezebel his wife came to him, and said to him, "Why is your spirit so sullen that you eat no food?" ⁶ He said to her, "Because I spoke to Naboth the Jezreelite, and said to him, "Give me your vineyard for money; or else, if it pleases you, I will give you another vineyard for it." And he answered, "I will not give you my vineyard."

⁷ Then, Jezebel, his wife said to him, "You now exercise authority over Israel! Arise, eat food, and let your heart be cheerful; I will give you the vineyard of Naboth the Jezreelite." ⁸ And she wrote letters in Ahab's name, sealed them with his seal, and sent the letters to the elders and the nobles who were dwelling in the city with Naboth. *⁹ She wrote in the letters, saying, Proclaim a fast, and seat Naboth with high honor among the people; ¹⁰ and seat two men, scoundrels, before him to bear witness against him, saying, You have blasphemed God and the king. Then take him out, and stone him, that he may die.*

¹¹ *So the men of his city, the elders, and nobles who were inhabitants of his city did as Jezebel had sent to them, as it was written in the letters which she had sent to them.* ¹² *They proclaimed a fast and seated Naboth with high honor among the people.* ¹³ *And two men, scoundrels, came in and sat before him; and the scoundrels witnessed against him, against Naboth, in the presence of the people, saying, "Naboth has blasphemed God and the king!" Then they took him outside the city and stoned him with stones so that he died.* ¹⁴ *Then they sent to Jezebel, saying, "Naboth has been stoned and is dead."* ¹⁵ *And it came to pass when Jezebel heard that Naboth had been stoned and was dead, that Jezebel said to Ahab, "Arise, take possession of the vineyard of Naboth the Jezreelite, which he refused to give you for money; for Naboth is not alive, but dead."* ¹⁶ *So it was when Ahab heard that Naboth was dead, that Ahab got up and*

went down to take possession of the vineyard of Naboth the Jezreelite.

In verse 7, Jezebel implies to Ahab that he essentially "owned" Israel and as far as she was concerned Israel and anything in it was his property. He had a right to the land to do with it as he pleased. This was a false belief on Jezebel's part but a shared conviction of one from a privileged background. It was this conviction that drove her to conspire against Naboth.

First, she wrote letters in Ahab's name (she forged his signature and usurped his authority). In the letter, she instructed the city elders and nobles in Naboth's home town to arrange a gathering where Naboth was to be the "special guest." Finally, she instructed them to arrange for two false witnesses to attend and give false testimony against Naboth. They would no doubt be willing to do this as Naboth represented all they hated as sons of Belial (SOBs) – those dedicated to darkness whose aim was to spread corruption and create the downfall of the nation. Many nations are experiencing the rise of these sons of Belial today.

The celebration in Naboth's honor turned into a Court of Hell for him as these elders and nobles followed the instructions of Queen Jezebel. Courts of Hell do not convene only in Hell. These elders were the judges of their city along with the nobles and were responsible to rightly judge on behalf of the people. Their fear of disobeying the queen induced them to conspire against Naboth resulting in his death by stoning. Jezebel then finalized this wicked deed by confiscating Naboth's property – land that was rightfully his heirs – and gave it to Ahab. By doing so she stole the livelihood from his family.

This series of events was the final straw in the downfall of Ahab as Elijah was immediately sent to Ahab to confront him. The kingdom would be ripped from him in a very violent manner which occurred not long after.

Throughout the Word of God, we can find three particular things that cry out for justice: innocent bloodshed, land that has been illegally seized, and wages that have been defrauded. In this story, we have an example of all three crying out at the same time: Naboth's innocent blood shed, the lost land, and the lost wages. With the property confiscated and the loss of income due to their vineyard being stolen (which was their livelihood) compounded by the failure to compensate his heirs for the value of the property – all these things resulted from Jezebel's wicked act.

Naboth's property also represented his inheritance. He could not sell it or get rid of it in any fashion. It had been distributed to him from his ancestors, and his duty was to share it with his seed when the time came. The cry for justice from the innocent bloodshed, the land, and the wages was intense. It got the attention of the Just Judge, and he responded by sending Elijah to notify Ahab of the coming judgment. Each of these items possesses its own judgment or consequence. Ahab had invited them all by allowing Jezebel to act wickedly against an innocent man.

This false title that Ahab now possessed to Naboth's land was an assertion of ownership from its rightful owner. Fortunately, we have the option of having these false ownership claims rectified in the Courts of Heaven in the Court of Titles and Deeds. Let's continue learning about this.

Chapter 2
Emotional Liens

Often we can allow deep emotions to place liens upon our life – loneliness, depression, despair, hopelessness, grief, et. al. These emotions try to own us. They dictate how we feel, what we do, how we respond to people. They can dominate our lives.

In one of the advocacy sessions in the Courts of Heaven we inquired of the Lord concerning what liens or false titles were working against the young lady we were representing. (We can inquire for ourselves or others as needed). We were sometimes surprised at the responses.

In this case a young lady was trapped by a lien of loneliness upon her life. We forgave her for embracing the lies the enemy used against her, blessed her, and released her. As we did freedom came. A sense of peace settled upon us as Holy Spirit witnessed the satisfaction of the lien.

[We will outline the typical procedure we use to bring people to freedom in this court in the QuickGuide near the end of this book.]

When you consider the ways that grief or worry can impact a person's life, it is apparent that it wants to take over their life. This becomes false ownership or a lien against them that must be satisfied in order to be released. For persons having recently experienced a significant loss of a loved one, a certain amount of grief is entirely natural. Yet when the grief paralyzes that person, and they are still consumed by the loss many months or even years later, it is more than just the normal amount of grief. The lien needs to be satisfied and if they have given themselves over to grief, they must experience a transfer of title back to the Lord Jehovah.

Stages of False Ownership

It seems that the false ownership scenario is created in stages. Here is how it works in relation to grief:

1) The event occurs and normal grief ensues.

2) When it is prolonged grief lasting many months or even years and although they may not have surrendered to it, they still feel entrapped by it, **a lien has been created**. The person needs to

be forgiven for embracing the grief to this degree, blessed, and released from it, thus satisfying the demands of the lien.

3) **When they give themselves wholly over to the grief, a false title (or note) has been created** and a fraudulent transfer of ownership has occurred. This needs to be undone in the Courts of Heaven. We do this by requesting that the counterfeit title is voided and requesting a Transfer of Title to the correct owner – the Lord Jehovah. In the case of a note, request a full cancellation of the trade that created the note.

Now, whether it is grief or some other emotion, the stages seem to be similar. The degree of surrender to the emotion seems to dictate whether we are looking at a lien or false title. These false titles are essentially false judgments, but since we are operating in the Court of Titles and Deeds, we will get them dealt with in this court. This can happen with any emotion and also occurs with health issues.

In one scenario, a person had a great sense of longing to see her children and grandchildren. She was unable to remedy the situation from a natural standpoint, so the longing had created a demand upon her soul in the form of a lien. She repented for embracing the lies involved, sought and received forgiveness and the lien was satisfied. The blood of

Jesus is always our highest answer to any lien or false title.

A principle we need to understand is this:

---

*What we focus on
becomes central to our life.*

*What is central to our life
will dictate our future.*

Whether it is the loss of a loved one, homesickness, a longing to be married (if you are single), depression – you name the emotion – if you focus on it long enough, it will consume you. Another way of saying it follows:

---

*What you feed will live and
what you starve will die.*

What are we feeding? What are we starving? That principle applies to many areas of our lives.

---

*A major purpose for the Court of
Titles and Deeds is to get proper
ownership issues settled.*

Chapter 3
Ties That Bind

Married couples around the globe have endured dysfunctional relationships without ever knowing the apparent root cause. In one scenario a woman had been married for forty years. As we inquired about outstanding liens or false titles, she immediately had a vision of her mother's hand reaching into her heart. The mother (though long dead) had never released her daughter to be a wife to her husband. She had not approved of the daughter's choice and for whatever reason held onto her daughter's heart for all those years. Once we were able to identify this issue and deal with it in the Court of Titles and Deeds incredible freedom came. This hold upon her heart was now broken and she was free to be her husband's wife. How many women have suffered the same type of thing? Freedom, however, is simple to obtain in the Courts of Heaven!

While dealing with this same family, we began working on behalf of the husband. When we inquired as before about outstanding liens or false titles, again a vision was given showing the hands of all his siblings holding on to his heart. This would indicate that the man's family had a continual hold upon his heart interfering with his ability to truly be a husband to his wife. We are familiar with the passage where Jesus points out:

> [4] *And He answered and said to them, "Have you not read that He who made them at the beginning 'Made them male and female,'* [5] *and said, 'For this reason* ***a man shall leave his father and mother and be joined to his wife, and the two shall become one flesh,****'?* [6] *So then, they are no longer two but one flesh. Therefore what God has joined together, let not man separate." (Matthew 19:4-6) (Emphasis mine)*

Again, how many couples have never been released from family ties that keep them from having a fulfilling marriage? Whether you agree with their choice of a mate or not, is not necessarily your business. You have a responsibility to not hold on to those God said to release.

Soul Ties

Soul ties can create liens or false titles that must be released. When emotionally you give yourself to another person, you create a soul tie that can have wonderful consequences in your life or may result in very negative consequences. When negative consequences are the result, freedom must be sought and obtained.

Again, you will proceed from this court, repent, seek forgiveness for invoking the soul tie in an ungodly manner and gain forgiveness allowing the lien to be satisfied or the false title eliminated. If lies were embraced in the process, repent of embracing the lies as well. With soul ties, the records created need to be expunged so they have no reference point in the memory. Ask the records to be expunged and burned with fire. Also request a cleansing of the DNA.

I Love You with All My Heart

Although this is a lovely sentiment it can, in the wrong setting, be instituted against a persons' life. They have created an allegiance and giving of ownership over to another that may not be the person God has intended for them to give their heart to. Upon a breakup in the relationship, the depth of the emotional trauma inflicted will likely become apparent. Again, repentance is required for giving your heart to the wrong person, or doing so out of the proper timing, seek and obtain forgiveness, forgive the other party for anything they may have done that is sin in this matter and bless and release them.

You're Mine

This declaration may be subconsciously saying, "You're my possession. I own you," or "she's mine and no one else can have her." If that is the underlying intent – to create an ownership scenario, particularly if they say, "you'll always be mine." then a lien or false title is likely to be involved. This is particularly true if the declaration is coming from a narcissistic individual or one who is simply controlling. Some control in a passive-aggressive manner, but regardless of how it is demonstrated, control is still control.

A recent illustration came very close to home and made the national news. The lady who cut our hair for several years experienced a tremendous tragedy. Her pregnant daughter was murdered (along with their two small children). The wife had just told her husband that she wanted to separate from him. He was not willing to positively deal with that scenario, and the end result was the murder of four lives (hers, the unborn child and the two young children). If he could not have her, then neither could anyone else.

Broken Engagements

When an engagement is broken off invariably, soul ties are in play, but possibly something a little further, particularly if they had engaged in a sexual relationship (even if not intercourse). In Jewish culture, engagement was a much deeper relationship than what we have in our western culture. However, Satan does not want to argue over the details; he wants to establish false ownership of the parties involved.

In paternalistic societies, this would likely be his claim that the former bride-to-be was the property of the man and therefore a false title is involved and a Transfer of Title is needed to free her from those legal restraints. In maternal societies where the man would take on the woman's identity, the reverse may occur. Transfer of Title (ownership) is again required to acquire freedom for them.

Parental Demands

In cases where the parents have demanded the child marry a particular person liens or false titles may also be involved. These demands of ownership may also be coming from the other party's parents or grandparents. Parents are often guilty of living their life through their children, and marriage is one of the avenues that this occurs. Simply inquire in the court as to the existence of outstanding liens or false titles and follow the procedure for freedom.

Many years ago I heard the story of a family whose children never married. When the father was on his deathbed, he made each child promise never to marry, but stay single and take care of their mother. This demand created a false title on each of these children. It is doubtful that it was the perfect will of God for each of these children to never marry. As a result of this misguided demand, destinies were altered, and children that should have been born were never conceived. Parents, be careful what you demand.

Consequences of Intercourse

When sexual intercourse is involved, it deepens the issue. You have given yourself wholly to another and if they are not your mate, or are no longer your mate, then that soul tie, the false title needs to be removed from your life. If you were involved in sexual intercourse or illicit sexual activity outside of the bonds of male to female marriage, then you have created the scenario whereby you are dealing with liens, notes and or false titles. The behavior must be repented of, and forgiveness sought and gained. Also, forgive the other party(ies), bless them, and release them. Remember, that when it comes to sexual sin, you must confess it to another living human being to be cleansed[2]. You are likely to have multiple liens or false titles as the result of sexual immorality. Each sexual partner created a lien or false title to which you have obligations. Deal with these as thoroughly as possible within the Court of Titles & Deeds.

Paul, the apostle, expands on this in the first letter to the Corinthians. Corinth was a crossroads city. It was a center for commerce from every direction. Not only did various goods pass through the city, but also every kind of wickedness. Although the believers had been redeemed from all these wicked deeds, they were being tempted to return. Paul firmly lays out the consequences for those participating in these unrighteous acts:

> *[9] Do you not know that the unrighteous will not inherit the kingdom of God? Do not be deceived. Neither fornicators, nor idolaters, nor adulterers, nor homosexuals, nor sodomites, [10] nor thieves, nor covetous, nor drunkards, nor revilers, nor extortioners will inherit the kingdom of God. [11] And such were some of you. But you were washed, but you were sanctified, but you were justified in the name of the Lord*

---

[2] Confess your trespasses to one another, and pray for one another, that you may be healed. The effective, fervent prayer of a righteous man avails much. (James 5:16)

Jesus and by the Spirit of our God. ^{12} All things are lawful for me, but all things are not helpful. All things are lawful for me, but I will not be brought under the power of any. ^{13} Foods for the stomach and the stomach for foods, but God will destroy both it and them. Now the body is not for sexual immorality but for the Lord, and the Lord for the body. (1 Corinthians 6:9-13)

By their surrender to these lifestyles, the enemy was laying claim to them – body, soul, and spirit. They had experienced a Transfer of Title, but not in a good way. Only through repentance can they be brought back and inherit the kingdom of God which had been God's original intent. They needed a Transfer of Title back to Jehovah and cancellation of every lien against them. They can find this in the Court of Titles and Deeds.

Release from Divorce

Often when one has gone through the painful process of divorce, they may have the legal paperwork of a divorce, but in their heart they still have a longing for their former partner. They also may be entrapped in the sexual knowing that comes from the marriage relationship. In many cases they feel as if their life has been put on hold and they cannot move forward. They need freedom from these things and within the Courts of Heaven is the solution: Request a Transfer of Title from the former spouse, thus freeing the divorced person from the hold upon their being and releasing them to go on with their life in joy and not sorrow. The cloak of heaviness will be lifted and they will be able to breathe again.

Chapter 4
Bondage of a Religious Flavor

People the world over have seen the excesses of some spiritual leaders over their flocks. Rather than feeding their flocks they are devouring them by their behavior and creating false ownership scenarios whereby the people are enslaved to that which is ungodly.

The last place we should be susceptible to evil agendas and actions should be within the church. We are just like the Jewish people throughout history, they have suffered at the hands of unrighteous leaders. They have contended with the ultra-religious Pharisees, Sadducees, and Scribes. Unfortunately, it is not different today. We have leaders acting as if they are God. They have their reward here. They will have none in Heaven supposing they get to Heaven.

Jesus warned us of the leaven of the Pharisees. Though we may not officially have Pharisees, we still do in many arenas unofficially. They create all kinds of hoops for us to jump through in order to please God. They want us to buy their latest teaching series and support their latest project or pay for a good prophetic word. We have criticized certain politicians for their "pay to play" schemes, but the leaders in the church are as guilty as they. Do we give preferred seats to the strongest givers and premium prophetic words to our greatest supporters? As James tells us in James 2, to show partiality in that way is a sin.

Victims are created within the church. We are induced to make covenants, vows, and oaths to them and to prove our undying allegiance by our faithful giving. Then we allow them to lay hands on us and impart something to us – however, what is imparted may be something we do not really need. The allegiances (when out of balance) create liens, notes or false titles that must be removed from our lives and families.

Laying Claim to the Flock

Some pastors lay claim to the flock under their care and refer to them as "their" flock. Some mean much more than as an identifier. Some go beyond merely a phrase of endearment, they attempt to take ownership. If you have been under this kind of leader, I expect you will find in your inquiry in the Court of Titles and Deeds that you do indeed, have an outstanding lien or false title with which you need to get released from.

---
*Unhealthy leaders
create unhealthy followers.*

Allegiance to the Man of God

Some leaders have even demanded that their parishioners lay on the ground so their feet would not have to touch "unholy" ground. Such demands are sickening and totally out of context with the whole of scripture. Others want you to always depend upon "their" anointing to get your miracle. Others want you to hang on to every word they speak. These are bondages and are not freeing in any measure.

---
*The demanded use of titles is a
flag of an unhealthy environment.*

If you are involved with a church that demands that you refer to the leader by a title such as pastor, apostle, or bishop (or whatever title is demanded), they are creating a false ownership system. The key word is *demanded.* To call someone by a title should be an act of courtesy and respect, and not done out of fear. It should be understood that the leader is not to be treated on the same level as your good friend and fishing buddy Bubba, but if the structure unequivocally demands that titles be used in every instance – run!

Jesus gave us a guideline in Matthew 23:8:

But you, do not be called "Rabbi"; for one is your Teacher, the Christ, and you are all brethren.

Prophetic Bondages

Uttered prophetic words with the intent to lay claim on a person or their anointing is problematic. Many lives have been taken off course due to the false hopes these false words invoked in their lives. The ensuing liens or false titles need to be released so the recipient can live free from those false words.

The people that claim that you MUST come under their headship to be successful in your Christian walk and to fulfill your destiny are to be avoided. It will have no good end. Deal with it in the Courts of Heaven.

If a church tells you that you will never reach your destiny if you ever leave, they are operating in a charismatic witchcraft. You do not need that in your

life. Make your exit and deal with the false ti[tles/]
liens involved.

Faulty Church Structures

Some church structures apart from the leader create false ownership structures. Some feel as if they are the ONLY "true" church. Every other church is apostate or some other baloney. If you are involved with a church such as this, do a checkup on yourself to see if any outstanding liens or false titles have been created against your life. You need to reconsider your involvement with that ministry.

> *Unhealthy churches can never produce healthy parishioners.*

Some would say that I am against church structure. I am not against godly church structure however I am wholeheartedly against abusive, life-destroying structures that have godless aims and godless ends. The body of Christ needs a major tune-up. We need some bad parts replaced with new ones. We need to be live-giving, not life-destroying.

Chapter 5
Medical Diagnoses

How many people become owned by a doctor's diagnosis of a persons' condition? When the prognosis is "terminal" it immediately seeks to "own" that persons' life. If we are talking about "the Big C," it certainly wants to take over your life. It comes complete with a package of fear, dread, and a host of other carpetbaggers. The expectation of chemo and radiation are enough to make the strongest heart among us struggle to stay strong.

It is crucial that these ownership situations be recognized so we can step over into freedom and remove our names from the list of those owned by "The Big C" and back to the list of those belonging wholly to the Lord.

Any "incurable" or chronic disease or condition will seek to own the patient. Whether they embrace that false ownership or not, is their decision. Yet to embrace the ownership of a condition is to also embrace the consequences of it. An arena to explore is how liens, notes or false titles may be impacting our ability to receive healing and restoration.

Casualty Covenants

We are often tricked into embracing false ownership. One such way is through casualty covenants. Holy Spirit explained it to me this way:

> *Suppose you were hearing someone testify of how God healed them of some disease and in the midst of his or her testimony, they are sharing what their symptoms were. As we nod in understanding hearing this wonderful testimony we may find ourselves thinking, "That sounds like what I have," or, "I've had those symptoms too!" In so doing we may inadvertently come to an agreement that what we are hearing is what we have experienced. Therefore, that must be the disease or condition we have.*
>
> *We have allowed a lien, note or false title to be enacted in our life and may find ourselves being diagnosed with the same disease the person testified concerning. It is very subtle, but also very effective on the part of the enemy. Sympathy can be a trap in these situations.*

If we have come into a casualty covenant like this, we need to repent and request a satisfaction of the lien or a Transfer of Title back to the Lord Jehovah Raphe – the Lord, our healer.

A casualty covenant was in play within my relatives a few years ago. A great uncle by marriage died on a specific date in September several years ago. Not long afterward, his son announced to his family that he felt he would die about that time of the year. He was all too correct in his prediction. Just a couple of years later he died almost to the day his father died.

It continues. His mother, my great aunt, declared she would die on the same day as her husband had died, too! And just a few short years later she died on the same date her husband had died. I have seen the tombstone testifying to the casualty covenants his mother, my aunt made. He was buried in another cemetery. Once they made that covenant they, in essence, surrendered title to their lives over to a spirit of death and he carried out their wishes.

Be aware of the power of casualty covenants to enact liens, notes or false titles in our lives and in the lives of those we love.

Chapter 6
Modern Day Slavery

The uptick in kidnappings of children and young people over the last couple of years is alarming. It has been revealed that very high-level occult practitioners and Satanists are committed to a minimum of one human sacrifice every hour of EVERY day. That is 24 lives sacrificed daily to create blood trades so that those offering the sacrifices can increase their devilish power.

One per hour is 168 sacrifices per week, over 700 per month and over 8,700 lives sacrificed per year. This is reaching epidemic proportions.

Some are kidnapped for purposes of human sacrifices, while others are kidnapped to become sex slaves. Gender is not the issue. Recent efforts have come to the forefront in trying to make pedophilia "normal" behavior. It is being referred to as someone who "prefers younger persons." These are your babies we are talking about, your grandchildren, your next door neighbor's child. Not only has a claim been made in the natural, but one has also been made in the realm of the spirit.

Globally it is estimated that more than 4.5 million persons are victims of sex-trafficking. In the United States, it has a major economic impact as an underground economy with an estimated $39 million impact in Denver, Colorado, but an astounding $290 million impact in Atlanta, Georgia.

The church has been asleep at the switch with this issue but is now beginning to awaken. The strategies in this book will be important tools to gain freedom for the victims of sex-trafficking. As our foes are first supernatural in nature, we must address that arena first. As we do, our impact and efforts can spill over to bring about needed changes in the natural arena.

Remember the story of Debbie at the beginning of this book. As the false ownership issue was dealt with in the courts, freedom could begin to be realized in the natural arena. So it will be with many of these future delivered captives as these false claims of ownership are rescinded in the Courts of Heaven by the Just Judge.

Freeing Nations and People Groups

Entire tribal peoples the world over are under false claims of ownership hindering their forward progress for them as a people and affecting their contributions to the world. Over the last two years, I have spent several weeks in the Indian state of Nagaland. The Nagas are a beautiful people with wonderful contributions to make to the nations of men. They are particularly a very musical people, and wonderful sounds are coming forth from the hills and valleys of Nagaland.

At the end of World War II, the British relinquished control of India and of Nagaland which had been its own separate people group. They had been promised by the British that they would be allowed to formulate their own nation separate from any other. In the larger scheme of things, the British reneged on their promise of independence and forced them to become a part of the newly formed independent nation of India. This was in spite of the invaluable assistance rendered by the Nagas toward the British during World War II and assurances of independence.

It was in Kohima, the capital of Nagaland that one of the most decisive battles of World War II was fought. The Japanese needed the resources of India in order to survive and advanced toward India from Burma through Nagaland. The battleground was Kohima and the Nagas, before, during, and after the battle provided tremendous amounts of assistance to the British and Indians in reconnaissance of the Japanese, guiding the British and Indian armies through the dense jungles, and providing labor and food to help in the effort to defeat the Japanese. Many Nagas died alongside British and Indian troops during the siege.

The decision to make Nagaland a state of Indian on the part of Britain had dire consequences for the Nagas. It was very short-sighted on the part of the British. The Nagas facial features are entirely unlike the balance of the Indian population. Nagas have oriental features as opposed to the very European facial structure of the majority of Indians. The British culture taught the Indians how to behave as a superior people group. When the British were in control of India, they were the superior people, and everyone else was subservient to them. With the British out of the way, the Indians took on that same attitude and thus behaved toward the Nagas the way the British had formerly behaved towards them. Deep racial divides were created between the Indians and Nagas.

Additionally, Hindu culture teaches that any tribal person is less than a dog. The Nagas were a tribal people, so this belief gave permission to India (and in particular to the occupying Indian Army) to do with the Nagas as they desired. The next sixty years were spent in a civil war between India and Nagaland with the Indian Army going to great lengths to destroy the Nagas. History records the mass destruction of tribes and villages, and gang rapes of the Naga women by entire troops of Indian Army soldiers. Thousands of lives were lost as a result. Only in recent years have the Nagas and Indians come to a cease-fire agreement. People groups such as the Nagas need to be freed in the realm of the spirit so they can reach their potential.

Oppressive Dictators

Oppressive dictators often declare their ownership of the people of their nation. We see that in North Korea, China, Cuba, and many other countries. Whereever you have an oppressive dictator, you have false titles in play. We need to begin effective courtroom work on behalf of the people of these nations.

Racism

In America, racism has been rearing its ugly head and causing much strife and division. It is recognized that throughout history whites have done horrific things to other races. Depending upon where you start, the same can be said about the dominant race on every continent. In the subcontinent of India, as just mentioned, the Indians have oppressed the Nagas. In South Africa, the blacks are oppressing the whites. In their history, the whites oppressed the blacks during apartheid. However, two wrongs never make a right.

Is it possible that false claims of ownership are at work creating and maintaining these divides? I believe the answer is yes. We need to deal with these false titles, notes or liens and get rightful ownership restored. In no culture are the whites to own the blacks, or the blacks to own the whites, the Indians to own the Orientals among them, and so on.

The earth is the Lord's and the fullness thereof; the people and all they that dwell therein. (Psalm 24:1)

Let us work to restore the peoples of the earth to their rightful owner – the Lord God Jehovah.

Chapter 7
The Court of Titles and Deeds

by Tracy Murillo

Author's Note: *This chapter is also in my book, "Engaging the Courts of Heaven." It will tell the story of our introduction to this particular court. Our first introduction involved land and property issues, but the Court of Titles and Deeds does far more than land issues. Enjoy!*

Do you have a property situation that needs to be dealt with in this court? Do you have land that will not sell? Do you know of a property that seems cursed? Do you know of an area where nothing seems to be successful on that particular site? Are you considering buying a piece of property? Do you know of someone who seems to be "owned" by the devil or one of his kids?

You should consider going to the Court of Titles and Deeds to know the status of any property you are considering. What needs to be dealt with before buying? Will it be a good investment? Should I go forward, or not?

———

Having been going to the Courts of Heaven for about four years, I was familiar with the Mercy Court. Within my heart, I knew the Courts of Heaven contained so much more to see and experience. When a friend asked me about going to the Courts of Heaven to petition about two properties she owned, I agreed to assist her. Although I was not sure how to handle properties, I trusted the Judge and Seven Spirits of God to lead us both. About a month later I traveled to her home where we stepped into the Courts of Heaven. At that time we gave the Just Judge her petitions.

The court opened in the usual way of asking everyone to be present and the blood to speak a word. After only a few minutes I noticed something was different about this court. Its walls were different. Small drawers lined the walls very much like deposit boxes in a bank. As I asked the Judge where we were, he said, "The Court of Titles and Deeds." I did not know such a place existed. But okay, I loved new things and treasures in Heaven.

It was then I proceeded to ask for more revelation. Two angels guarded each drawer. We brought one of the two properties to the attention of the Judge. As we gave the address, an angel went to a specific drawer and pulled out a rolled paper and took it to the Judge. A funny thing happened. As the Judge unrolled the scroll, the land depicted on the paper became alive. It was like watching a movie. It played out every day on that land from the beginning as if in fast forward. We saw varioius special events that had been held on that property. We heard and saw the sights and sounds of rejoicing and celebrations. It was beautiful. Flowers were everywhere. We watched for a long while and then asked for more revelation.

As soon as we asked for more revelation, everything changed. The land became dark, and many men appeared shackled in chains singing an old hymn. I wondered what had happened. We had asked for revelation about anything holding the land captive. We could tell by the clothes and chains it was definitely during the slave trading era of the United States. As we continued to watch the vision, some were being beaten and sold into slavery. Most, if not all, had suffered mistreatment and now did not know their fate. Many were suffering from malnutrition and were weak from the long journey. We could feel the anguish and heartbreak of these people. We could also sense the unrighteous deeds that were done on that property. My friend began to repent on behalf of the landowner for allowing such tragedies to happen on that property. It seemed that they would bring the slaves from the ships and sell them at that place. We then felt impressed to ask the Judge for the release of every slave that had been chained. We also requested they be released from the hatred and unforgiveness in their hearts due to such treatment. We then repented for their families allowing the hate to go on down into future generations. Soon after that we heard and saw the chains falling off the prisoners; they were free! It was amazing to observe, and we were very much feeling their freedom in ourselves.

As we asked for more revelation, we began to see that the land was alive and beautiful again. All the slaves were gone and it appeared as a pretty sunny meadow. The families from the former place in time had been set free. The land was set free. As we watched, the Judge rolled up the paper and stamped it, "Approved." Then he had the angel return the document to the proper drawer for safe keeping. My friend knew in her heart that now the land was hers and she could do with it as the Lord deemed for her family.

A few months later, we decided to take the second piece of property into the courts. As we entered the Courtroom, we could tell that we were once again in Court of Title and Deeds. The small drawers were everywhere, so we proceeded to usher everyone in and ask for the Judge to open the Court. We gave an angel the address of the property. Again an angel went to a drawer, brought out a rolled up paper, and presented it to the Judge. We asked for revelation for this property because it was in a different state. Soon after the document was rolled out on the table, the land came to life again. It showed the history of the property and a movie began to play very much like in the prior court setting. Everyone in the Courtroom watched the celebrations, weddings, babies being born, and the lifetime of this property.

We asked for the Seven Spirits of God to guide us and lead us to the curses that might be here as well. I learned that because someone gives you property it is not yours until the Just Judge says it is. We then asked what was holding it. I began to see a woman burying gold coins into the ground in several places and wondered what that meant. Was she trying to save money for her family? A lot of people would hide their fortunes in the ground rather than putting them in a bank. After asking the question, I sensed "no." This was something else. I then saw my friend and her grandson going around the property digging up coins. I told her what I was seeing, and I asked my friend what she thought that meant? Had she or her family buried money or gold coins anywhere on the land? She said no.

As we continued, we felt that the coins being placed in the ground were not right. She would indeed begin to look for them in the natural. I then had a brief picture of my friend receiving the answer about what all this meant. We asked the Judge and felt like that was all for now about this property. We then saw a picture of her daughter running all over the property with stakes very much like the movie "Far and Away." She was claiming all the land for their family. It was so exciting! Even though we didn't understand about the coins, we felt the property would be released for my friend. We asked for a continuance and left the courtroom.

Two weeks later my friend received an email from her sister-in-law. The sister-in-law disclosed she had met with a medium who told her to place coins in the ground on the land. Once she did that the property would sell. My friend was shocked. A medium had cursed the land and her sister-in-law had agreed to it. Her sister-in-law would not tell her where the coins were buried. So my friend asked for revelation about where the coins were. She knew now that what we saw in court was correct and the coins were linked to darkness and curses.

The woman went everywhere on the property with a metal detector. They only found some pennies but felt such a relief to know that the Judge was breaking that agreement by revealing this to her. After removing the coins, they discovered such a sense of peace that it was done. She called me and told me the whole story and was so blessed that the Courts of Titles and Deeds had not only brought great revelation and freedom for her land, but had also increased her faith. These courtrooms are real and will bring answers to us if we believe and engage them.

This court is not limited to merely the ownership issues of lands and houses but also can extend to the ownership of people in many forms. Some people have literally been purchased as a possession of others. We often think of the sex-slave trade, but it extends further than that alone.

When someone has upon them a claim of ownership that is not the Lord, a Transfer of Title may be required to get them free and restored to his or her rightful owner. In Psalm 24:1, the Lord lays claim to the earth and all who dwell in it.

The earth is the Lord's, and all its fullness, the world and those who dwell therein.

Therefore, every inhabitant of this planet can rightfully be claimed as the property of the Lord of Hosts. This concept extends beyond this as well. Some (as a result of witchcraft, sorcery, and occult programming) have had their souls fragmented and scattered to the far parts of the universe – to the distant stars, planets, and constellations. Since Jehovah God is the creator of all, EVERYTHING belongs to Him – regardless of where it has been taken captive. The request for a Transfer of Title or cancellation of any false title, note or lien against someone's person or property needs to be requested. The blood of Jesus ransomed EVERY human that has ever lived.[3] Then seek the restoration of every fragmented part of their soul to be brought back to them. Finally, we enter the Court of Times and Seasons, requesting that their whole being be brought into alignment with the timing and purposes of God.

Do you have a property situation that needs to be dealt with in this court? Do you have land that will not sell? Do you know of a property that seems cursed? Do you know of a land or region where nothing seems to be successful? Are you considering buying a piece of property? Should you consider going to the courts to know the status of that property? What needs to be dealt with before buying? Will it be a good investment?

To apply this to what we have discovered recently in this court, simply access the court and make the inquiry about any outstanding liens, notes or false titles affecting the property, then respond

---

[3] 1 Timothy 2:5-6 For there is one God and one Mediator between God and men, the Man Christ Jesus, [6] who gave Himself a ransom for all, to be testified in due time,

accordingly. You can use the QuickGuide in the next chapter as a tool for a head start.

Chapter 8
QuickGuide for the
Court of Titles & Deeds

This chapter will guide you through a typical procedure for bringing someone to freedom from outstanding liens, notes or false titles. Although I hesitate to produce this because some will make this a hard and fast method, that is not my intent. I have found that if I can provide you a loose guide that it will help you learn the basics until you are able to do this on your own. When using any of the QuickGuides, I produce they are only jump starters. (See www.courtsofheavenbook.com for additional resources)

We step into the realms of Heaven (see Chapter 11 for how to do this).

We ask permission to access the Court of Titles and Deeds and ask:

Are any outstanding liens, false titles or notes active against _____'s life?

Await the answer. Typically: a "yes" or "no."

What do these involve?

Await a description, word, or picture. Often it will be only a word or two or a simple image.

The person(s) responsible created bondage for the person we are representing in court. The offending party has sinned against them, and we must forgive them (John 20:23[4]). At this point we do the following:

*Your honor, we choose to forgive _____. We **forgive** them, we **bless** them[5], and we **release**[6] them from this sin and its penalties.*

If the issue was a sin committed, then:

Your honor I confess my sin of _____ and repent and ask your forgiveness. I ask that the blood of

---

[4] John 20:23 If you forgive the sins of any, they are forgiven them; if you retain the sins of any, they are retained.

[5] Luke 6:27-28 But I say to you who hear: Love your enemies; do good to those who hate you, [28] bless those who curse you, and pray for those who spitefully use you.

[6] Luke 4:18 The Spirit of the Lord [is] upon Me, because He has anointed Me [the Anointed One, the Messiah] to preach the good news (the Gospel) to the poor; He has sent Me to announce release to the captives and recovery of sight to the blind, to send forth as delivered those who are oppressed [who are downtrodden, bruised, crushed, and broken down by calamity]. (AMP)

Jesus cover this sin now and ask you to release me from its penalty. I ask that any trades involved be completely cancelled in my behalf, in Jesus' name.

If you have embraced a lie or traded and eand it caused this lien or false title to come into play, then:

Your honor, I repent for embracing the lie that brought this situation into my life. I ask for your forgiveness and ask that this situation be remedied in my life.

Often you will sense a release. Once you feel this portion is complete, ask the following question:

Are any other false titles, notes or liens active against this person?

Again, await the answer and follow the procedure in the previous paragraphs. Finally, you will ask:

Are any other false titles, notes or liens active against this person?

[Typically I will limit the number of false titles, notes or liens that we are dealing with to possibly 5 or 6 at a time. We will deal with them and then return to continue the query.]

If you make the query about additional liens, notes or false titles and get a "no," or you get no response. At that point, make your request to the Judge.

Your honor, I request that every false title be invalidated, every lien be marked satisfied, and every note be satisfied that has been against _____ 's life.

As you observe the Just Judge, you may see him pouring through papers and signing or marking them in some way. He may stamp them and hand them off to a bailiff for distribution to the angels in the Court of Angels.

[In the event the Just Judge does not hand the paperwork to the bailiff, then you will step into the Court of Records and receive the paperwork, then deliver it to the Court of Angels for distribution.]

[You will often find that Holy Spirit has already hinted that He will be dealing with a particular issue by bringing it to their mind in the days immediately preceding the court session.]

You are not finished yet, however. Whenever someone (or some entity) has placed a lien, note or enacted a false title, it invariably creates situations where their life has been thrown off track. They may feel as if their life is "off-schedule." We want that corrected, and God has wonderfully provided the means to make that happen...via the Court of Times and Seasons. We will cover that procedure shortly, but first, we need to cover a variation of the steps we generally take in this court. Use the process chart when helping others in the courts.

Available at: www.courtsofheavenbook.com

COURT OF TIMES & SEASONS PROCESS-PERSON

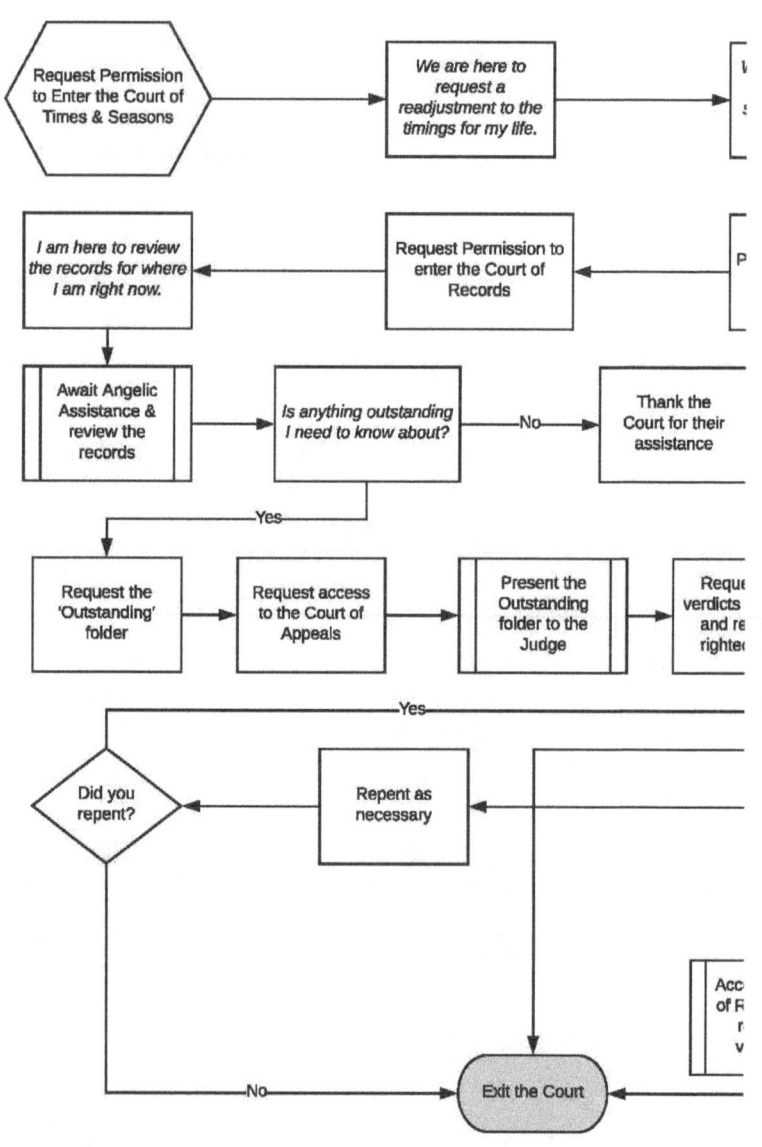

- Request Permission to Enter the Court of Times & Seasons
- We are here to request a readjustment to the timings for my life.
- Request Permission to enter the Court of Records
- I am here to review the records for where I am right now.
- Await Angelic Assistance & review the records
- Is anything outstanding I need to know about? —No→ Thank the Court for their assistance
- Yes
- Request the 'Outstanding' folder
- Request access to the Court of Appeals
- Present the Outstanding folder to the Judge
- Request verdicts and re... righte...
- Yes
- Did you repent? ←— Repent as necessary
- No → Exit the Court

Copyright ©2018 Dr. Ron M. Horner | All rights reserved (090418)

66

AL Dr. Ron M. Horner | www.courtsofheavenbook.com

```
[We ask that the timing of my life be synchronized with the timing of the Lord.] → [Watch & Listen for what is happening. You should see or sense angelic activity on your behalf as the timings for your life are adjusted.]
                                                        ↓ No
[Proceed to the Court of Records] ←—Yes— <Did you sense the timing was reset?>

                    (Exit the Court of Records)

[...est the false ...be overturned ...placed with ...us verdicts] → <Were verdicts rendered?> —Yes→ <Were verdicts given to the bailiff?>
                          ↑                                                                    ↓ No
         —————Yes——————                                              [Thank the Court for their assistance] ←—No—
         —————No———————                                                      ↓
[...ess Court ecords & ...ceive ...erdicts] → [Thank the Court for their assistance] → [Access the Court of Angels for dispatch]
```

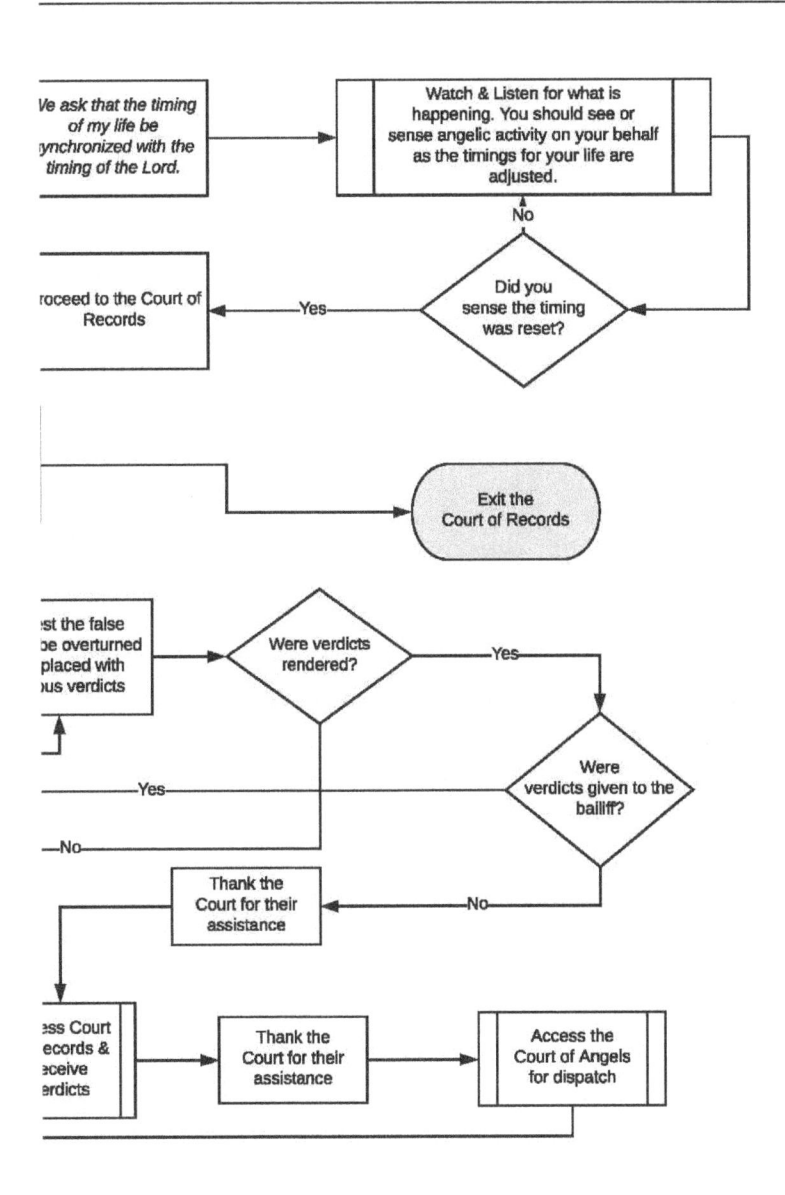

67

Chapter 9
Correcting Time

To everything there is a season, a time for every purpose under heaven. (Ecclesiastes 3:1)

The Lord in his incredible wisdom has provided a means to get our lives on track. Often we get thrown off-track by situations, sicknesses, traumas, and events – and yes, by sin. When that occurs, we need that incorrect time corrected. For that, we access the Court of Times and Seasons. Within this court lost years can be erased and we can get our lives in synchronization with God's timing for us. At other times we have gotten ahead of God's timing and need our "clock" turned back to get in sync with God's timetable for our lives.

Certain things in our lives have specific points in time in which they are supposed to happen. When interferences to that set time come into our lives, it can create a cascading effect of missed opportunities, missed relationships, and missed blessings. Much like the troubles one can face if they miss their airline flight and their trip had connecting flights. We miss one flight, and it causes us to miss the next flight and so on.

On a recent trip with a team to India weather in the New York area was delaying our departure in Charlotte, North Carolina. We were told the trip was being delayed by an hour or so when that time came and went, we were told another targeted time. That came and went. All the while our layover time was disintegrating a moment at a time. We had given ourselves 3-4 hours of layover time in-between flights. We had an international connection to make and the time for its departure was fast approaching. Finally, we were allowed to board the plane for our flight, only to be informed that we had to disembark because the flight was canceled. They announced the flight was then canceled. Our window of time to make the trip to Newark, New Jersey was gone.

Now we had to make arrangements for another flight to our final destination. We booked with another airline, but the flight was not scheduled to leave until the next day. We had to arrange hotel rooms in order to stay overnight. Meanwhile, our luggage was still on the plane. That original flight eventually did take off to Newark...complete with all our luggage. Now we are heading to a hotel for an overnight stay with no luggage. Fortunately for me, I had a change of clothes in my carry-on bag, but the other team members did not.

---
*Word of Wisdom:
Always pack a change of clothes
in your carry-on*

Missing the first flight caused us to miss the second flight. The scheduled pick up for us in New Delhi was missed as well. This one event – originally a weather delay caused a whole series of events.

Yes, we did arrive a day later in New Delhi. Our scheduled recovery day had disappeared, and we immediately had to begin our seminar with no time to recover – all without our luggage, too!

Two days later our luggage arrived. Hallelujah! Right timing is important. Some situations have specific windows of time in which to happen. We must be on track to make the connection.

In other situations, we are ahead of the timing of the Lord. One of the strategies of the enemy is to push us to do things before either we or others (or other things) are ready. To be ahead of time also can result in negative repercussions. Many times ministry assignments you may have are co-dependent. Others are to play a vital part, but they haven't arrived at that particular point in time, or the resources needed have yet to arrive, or the venue is not ready.

When Solomon wrote, "there is a time for every purpose under Heaven," he was saying far more than we realize. Often those times are precise with little leeway for the intersection of all the pieces.

You may say, "But can't God just shift things around and make it happen?" Possibly, but should He? We sometimes want him to bail us out and excuse our disobedience or lack of sensitivity to what He is doing. Just as an earthly father should not always bail their children out of situations, so our Heavenly Father does not bail us out of some situations. We need to learn the lesson of full obedience.

The "process" we follow to get timings readjusted is simple – wonderfully simple. We will outline it here and illustrate it with a few examples from our experiences.

We ask permission to enter the Court of Times and Seasons, and upon receiving permission, we step in. You may be aware of the many clocks in the court, or of the sound of the ticking of clocks. It is as if you have entered the shop of a Master Clock Repairer. I have sensed the tick-tock sounds, the ticking sounds of all types of clocks...even clocks that are linear in shape and not round as is typical. Some have seen clocks with various time zones represented or names of countries above the clock.

We announce,

We are here in regard to a readjustment of time for _____.

We ask that the timing of their life be synchronized with the timing of the Lord.

We watch and listen.

At this point, the Lord will have angels begin working on adjusting a clock relating to the person involved. Just observe and wait for a signal of finality – the clock clicking into place, or aligning to the 12 o'clock position, or something similar. You may hear, "It's done!"

An example:

In one of my early forays into this court, we were aware of the many clocks but were drawn to one particular Grandfather Clock. As we watched it, we noticed a procession of angels marching in cadence in military formation. They came close to where we were standing and stopped. One of the angels stepped out of formation, walked over to the Grandfather clock and opened the door on the face of the clock. He then took his finger and gently moved the minute hand back a few minutes. He closed the door on the face of the clock and then opened the long door at the bottom where the weights and chains are for rewinding the clock were. He pulled on the chains to rewind the clock, closed the door, stepped back into formation, and the angels left. Immediately my friend heard, "She's on schedule now!"

On another occasion we were in this court, only the scene was slightly different. We saw a clock, and once we had asked for the readjustment of time for this person, we saw the hands spinning furiously ahead. This person's life had been seriously impacted by some poor decisions years ago. As a result they had gotten off-track with the timing of the Lord. After spinning rapidly for a few moments, the hands began to slow down and finally got to the 12 o'clock marker and we heard a loud click. They were now settled into their right timing.

On a couple of occasions I have seen a clock that appeared linear. We stepped into the court on behalf of a woman and saw this clock laying on a surface. This clock had a series of gears and bars (I don't know how else to describe it). Suddenly a group of angels appeared with all kinds of tools and began prying and pushing and pulling on some of the parts. One angel came with a large hammer and began to bang on a part. It was as if the parts of the clock had rusted and could no longer move freely. After several swings with the hammer, a part broke free of the rust-like substance and slid into place. Another part was not quite in alignment, so he took his hammer and pounded it like a mechanic trying to nudge a part into its proper place. After a few minutes of watching this rather comical scene, the parts were freed up and came into sync with one another. The clock began to work properly again.

In this woman's life a traumatic event had occurred several years before and in that arena of her life, she had felt stuck. This visit to the Court of Times and Seasons resulted in her becoming "un-stuck" from this event and could now move ahead freely.

In another scenario, the clock raced backward and stopped. In still another, it ran forward. Often the illustration of clocks hands racing around is a good illustration of what is happening in the spirit. We have to remember that the realm of the spirit is outside of time. Time is for our benefit, so we know to rest our bodies and souls. It gives order to our lives and helps us keep our lives in order.

In our work in this court we have also seen changing of seasons involved. In one case, as we stepped in we were aware of the changing from winter to spring in the person's life. We then watched as several clocks were adjusted for them.

In yet another instance while the clocks were being reset by the hands spinning rapidly around, we were also aware that the seasons were rapidly changing as well. We could sense going from spring to summer to autumn on to winter continuously for several cycles while at the same time the clocks themselves were being reset. Apparently this person's life had been severely impacted and needed major readjustments in order to be in their proper alignment for the plans of the Heavenly Father.

In all these illustrations we had first been to the Court of Titles and Deeds to take care of the liens, and false titles. It is wonderful to see the infinite variety of ways the Lord readjusts peoples timing.

Once we have listened for what the Lord is doing in the court, we wait. For one lady she heard the clock click loudly at 12:00 – signifying the synchronization of the life and the timing was complete. On another occasion the clock had been reading nearly 12:00 and was reversed to 11:33. It has been our experience that when the person's clock settled at the 12:00 hour it was indicative of their clock being reset.

Whether you hear, see or just "know" follow the peace that will accompany the situation. You will simply have a sense or knowing that what you requested has been done.

Once the syncing is complete, we thank the court for helping with this issue and exit the courtroom. However, we are not done just yet. We still have somewhere else to go.

Chapter 10
What Do I Do Now?

Now that we are in a new place and our ownership issues have been resolved, we are now perfectly set into the timing of the Lord. We need to know what we are to do next. We have not been in this place before – it is entirely new, and the Lord has provided a magnificent solution.

We can access the Court of Records (aka Court of Scribes) and ask to see the books concerning where we are right now. We will walk through this in a few moments, but the following information will illustrate it beautifully.

In order to help us learn the Court System of Heaven, the Just Judge has provided a straightforward means of aiding us – a Help Desk. As we are learning to maneuver in the courts, we can just step up to the help desk and describe the issue to the attendant. Then ask, "Where should I go to deal with this?"

Often they (or another angel) will come forth and escort you to the appropriate court. The Courts of Heaven complex is like a large mall with a large central corridor with the various courts off to either side. Once you arrive at the appropriate court, another angel will be available to assist you.

As I explained this scenario recently to Katherine, she immediately began to engage the Help Desk. She explained her situation and asked for assistance.

The angel took her by the hand and escorted her down a large corridor. The ceiling was extremely high, and large rooms were on either side of the corridor. The angel brought her to a room that was on the right side. She could see lots of books in the room. I asked her to look above the door for the sign that would tell her where she was. It read, "Court of Records."

She stepped in, and another angel asked, "May I help you?" Again, she explained that she needed to see her book for where she was right now. The angel escorted her down an aisle and stopped at a shelf with some books and a large box. Katherine intuitively knew this was information for her. She took the box down from the shelf and saw in it what appeared to be USB sticks like you would use with a computer. She could merely touch one and a video would begin to play. She saw that it had a Fast Forward button, a

Rewind button, and a Play button. She could also pause the video to get a closer look at something or someone in the video.

As she played a particular video, she recognized someone and knew instinctively she was to meet with them and share some things concerning the Courts of Heaven. She had been hesitant to share things before because she felt she lacked sufficient understanding, but with all the court experiences she had this particular day she felt competent to share her experiences about the Help Desk. It was an instructional visit to the Court of Records and showed her a present assignment.

When she felt she had seen what she needed to see, the angel took the box and put it back on the shelf. They walked back outside where the original escort was waiting for her.

Previously I shared about the clock that moved forward very rapidly for a long period of time. That involved a man who had made some poor decisions years before that had dramatically affected his life and his family. In working with his wife in the courts, we accessed his book concerning the time in his life when the events first occurred. We had already been in the Court of Titles and Deeds and got proper ownership reestablished proper ownership in his life and were now requesting to see his book for where he "now" was.

As his wife saw his book, she saw pages and pages of negative events being erased. She had a knowing that even events where they (as a family) should have had great times of joy - those times were going to be restored.

In his case, the books were being erased all the way back to the time of the first wrong decision and being re-written for his life and his family. The joy that came forth from knowing the Lord was erasing the past and granting a new future was immense. Only the Lord can delete our history and give us new futures. He can make situations that had been bad as if they had never existed.

The implications for this occurring in people's lives are immense. Your past does not have to dictate your future. It is as if he took a video of your life and cut out the bad parts and re-rendered the video in such a way you don't even have memories of the bad times, or if you can recall them, the sting or pain in your heart they formerly caused is gone.

> [18] *Do not remember the former things, nor consider the things of old.* [19] *Behold, I will do a new thing, now it shall spring forth; shall you not know it? I will even make a road in the*

wilderness and rivers in the desert. (Isaiah 43:18-19)

Then He who sat on the throne said, "Behold, I make all things new." (Revelation 21:5)

He can place you exactly where you need to be at precisely the right time so you can move forward with your life.

Redeeming* the time, because the days are evil. (Ephesians 5:16)

Walk in wisdom toward those who are outside, redeeming* the time. (Colossians 4:5)

*The word translated "redeeming" means "to rescue from losses," or "to buy back." The Lord is able to cause that to be so in our lives.

On another occasion, we were given access to someone's box and in it were file folders. One was marked "Outstanding." We felt instructed to take it out of the box. We were then instructed by our assisting angel in that court to take it to the Court of Appeals because it contained some false judgments that needed to be dealt with by that person.

In addition, we were told to take out a Requisition Form. It was a requisition for finances and it had the current date written on it. We were instructed to complete it and submit it with the "Outstanding" file folder in the Court of Appeals.

We completed our work in the Court of Records and took the "Outstanding" file folder with us and were escorted to the Court of Appeals.

We found the court ready for our appearance. The man with the file folder walked up to the judge's bench and handed the file folder to the judge. The Judge opened the folder and began to read through it. He looked up from the paperwork and asked what he wanted the court to do about the items in the folder. He requested that the false verdicts would be overturned and replaced with righteous verdicts and that restitution would be made where appropriate. He also requested additional help for his wife concerning a situation.

The judge nodded and said, "Petition granted." We handed him the requisition form also and thanked him for his assistance. After stamping and signing the papers He handed them to the bailiff for recording and dispatch by the angels, and we left the courtroom.

In all these events we were aware that we were working within the realms of Heaven. In the next chapter, I will talk about learning to access these heavenly realms in order to maximize your work in the Courts of Heaven.

Chapter 11
Accessing
the Realms of Heaven

Author's Note: This chapter is from my book "Engaging the Courts of Heaven." It is essential that we understand how to access Heaven as we operate in the various Courts of Heaven. This chapter will help you to engage more fully in the Courts of Heaven.

A tremendous privilege we share in this time in history is the ability to access the realms of Heaven with ease. Many of us were taught that Heaven is only for after you die. Heaven is much more than a final destination on a journey, but also can be a vital aspect of that journey.

What I am about to share is vital in progressing in the various Courts of Heaven. We can access the Mercy Court (see the next chapter) while fully planted here on the earth, but to maximize our endeavors in the Courts of Heaven, we need to learn how to operate FROM Heaven.

In teaching on accessing the realms of Heaven, I often point out some simple facts. If you were to tell me you were a citizen of a particular town, but you could tell me little about it, I would have a tendency to doubt the authenticity of your citizenship. I am a citizen of a small town in central North Carolina. I am familiar with the location of the City Hall, Police Station, hospital, local county courthouse, Sheriff's Department and much more. I know where many sporting events will be held. I know where the parks are. I know many of the stores and restaurants. I am familiar with this small town. Yet, if I were to ask the average believer what they can describe of Heaven from personal experience, the answer will likely be – nothing. They have no personal knowledge of Heaven that they can relate to me. It does not have to be like that.

In Matthew 3, Jesus informed us that the Kingdom of Heaven was at hand. You could say, "the Kingdom of Heaven is as close as your hand." Hold your hand up in front of your nose as close as you can. Do not touch your nose. Heaven is closer to you than that. It is not far, far away up in the sky. It is not "over yonder" as some old hymns describe. It is a very present reality separated from us by a very thin membrane – and we can access it by faith. It is very simple.

When Jesus was baptized in the River Jordan, as he came up out of the water IMMEDIATELY the heavens were opened. He both saw (a dove) and heard (a voice coming from Heaven). That one act of Jesus restored our ability to access Heaven. We can experience open Heavens over our life. We don't have to wait. We can live conscious of the realm of Heaven and live out of that reality!

Everything we do as believers we must do by faith. Accessing the realms of Heaven is done the same way. In Chapter 5, I spoke of how prophetic acts can create realities for us. It is the same with this. You can visualize stepping from one room into another easily. It is like stepping from one place to another. To learn to access the realms of Heaven, you will follow the same pattern.

Stand up from where you are now and prepare to work with me. You can experience the realms of Heaven right now! You don't have to wait until you are dressed up in a long box at the local funeral home or decorating an urn. You can experience Heaven while you are alive!

Quiet yourself down. Turn off distracting background noises if possible. Prepare to relax and focus. Now, say this with me:

Father, I would like to access the realms of Heaven today. So right now, by faith, I take a step into the realms of Heaven. [As you say that, take a step forward.] Imagine you are going from one place to another in a single step. Once you have done so, pay attention to what you see and hear. You may see very bright lights; you may see a river, a pastoral scene, a garden – any number of things. You, right now are experiencing a taste of Heaven. You will notice the peace that pervades the atmosphere of Heaven. You might notice the air seems electric with life. The testimonies I've heard are always amazing and beautiful to hear.

Now spend a few minutes in this place. Remember, Jesus said to enter the Kingdom you must come as a little child. I often coach people to imagine yourself as an 8-year-old with what you are seeing. What would an 8-year-old do? He or she would be inquisitive and ask, "What is this? What does that do? Where does that go? Can I go here?" If a child saw a river or a lake, what would that child want to do? Most would want to jump in the water.

The variety is infinite. The colors – amazing! The sounds are so beautiful. You can learn to do this on a regular basis. When you access the realms of Heaven, you are home. You were made to experience the beauty that is Heaven.

The reason learning to access the realms of Heaven is crucial to engage the Courts of Heaven. Much of what we do is done FROM Heaven, so we need to learn to engage Heaven and work from it.

Many people tell me they can't "see" visually in the spirit. Often they are discounting the ability they do have. They may be discounting their "knower." Every believer has a "knower" at work within them. This "knower" who is Holy Spirit at work within you helps you perceive things. Whether something is good or evil, He works to guide you more than you may have realized. Most navies with submarines have a device known as sonar. Sonar gives a submarine "eyes" to see what is in their vicinity. They can detect by the ping the sonar gives what the object is. They can determine the distance to the object and if it is another submarine. They can even identify what class of submarine it might be. A video camera would be rather useless underwater.

The military has a similar device for above ground situations known as radar. It functions in the same manner. If a pilot were flying through thick cloud cover, the pilot would need to know what is in his path. Radar becomes his eyes.

Some people function visually. They often see what amounts to pictures or video images when they "see" in the spirit. They may see more detail. Yet one operating by his or her "knower" (their spiritual radar or sonar) can be just as effective as a seer. If you operate more like sonar/radar, don't discount what you "see" in that manner. It is how I function and I have been doing this type of work for many years.

I can often detect where an angel is in the room or if it is one of the men or women in white linen. I can often detect how many are present and whether they have something they are to present to someone. I can detect any number of things and even though it is not "visual," it is still "seeing." Understanding that operating by your knower is as valid as any other type of vision will set your mind at ease. It will help you to realize you have seen much more than you know and you may know much more than some who only see.

As you practice accessing the realms of Heaven you are beginning a wonderful adventure that will bless your life in amazing ways. Enjoy the journey!

Chapter 12
The Court of Records
or
Court of Scribes

Author's note: Chapter 12 and 13 are modified slightly from my book, "Engaging the Courts of Heaven." The terms "Court of Records" and "Court of Scribes" speak of the same court. I shall use "Court of Records" most often.

Now that you have the decision from the judge, what do you do next? Once a decision is rendered, you need the resulting paperwork. The solution is simple. The Courts of Heaven has a Court of Records wherein records of court proceedings are recorded and kept. It also contains the records of your life...everything you are to do, everything you have done, every word you have spoken is on record here. Throughout this book I will use these terms interchangeably. The angels will make those papers available to you. (In the American court system we have a Clerk of Courts office performing similar functions). As I enter this court I will say something like:

> *I ask permission to enter the Court of Records today.*

You will likely have a sense that it OK to proceed. As you step into the Court of Records (often these "papers" will be in the form of scrolls). You simply ask for a copy of the paperwork from your case to be given to you. I usually say something like this:

> *I have come seeking the scroll(s) of the verdict just received in the Court of Titles and Deeds (or whatever court you were just in).*

Hold out your hands as if to receive this scroll or book. You may sense (or see) a scroll. It often takes the form of a scroll or a book. You can read it, but now that you have the paperwork you need to engage the next court. You need to get angels activated to carry out the instructions mandated in those scrolls. We will discuss that shortly, but first, let us examine the ways the verdicts manifest.

As I mentioned they often take the shape of a scroll or a book. These books often look like the old books you would find in the Deed Vault of your local county courthouse. If in the shape of a scroll, understand that both terms: scrolls and books are often used in the Bible. Many times you will see something written or stamped on the outside of the scroll. I have seen words on various scrolls or books in that court: Cleansed, Healed, Free, Approved, Not Guilty, and more; any variety of words describing the contents of the scroll.

At other times they manifest as sheets of paper like the papers you would receive from the Clerk of Court's office. Sometimes you do not "see" but sense or perceive the paperwork in whatever form it happens to be in.

These papers include the directives of the court relating to your petition in the court you were in previously. It may be an order of the court releasing angels to minister to your children, or an order releasing funds for a particular situation, or authorizing certain things be done in your behalf. Any number of things can be in these papers or scrolls.

On a number of occasions, multiple scrolls were issued about a court case. The sense was as if someone loaded his or her arms with a stack of firewood. At times the person could feel the weight of the scrolls in their arms as they carried them.

Yet, having the orders is one thing. Seeing that the orders or instructions are carried out is a different matter. For that, we are going to need angelic help, and with that, we will now proceed to the Court of Angels.

NOTE: On occasion the Judge will hand the paperwork directly to an angel serving as a bailiff who takes the paperwork directly to the Court of Records and to then to the Court of Angels for dispatch by the angels. The rule of thumb I follow is that if I don't see the Judge hand the paperwork to an angel, then I proceed to the Court of Records to receive the scrolls.

If I do see the Judge hand off the paperwork to an angel, I know that I am finished and I thank the court for hearing the case and exit.

Chapter 13
The Court of Angels

Upon receiving the paperwork from the Court of Records, it is now time to get the verdict enforced. This is where angelic help occurs.

In Hebrews 1:14 we read:

Are they [angels] not all ministering spirits sent forth to minister for those who will inherit salvation?

That's us! The angels are ready and waiting to work on our behalf. As you go through this process, imagine yourself being in a place like I am describing. Imagine yourself handing out the papers or orders to the angels or having them take them from your hands. These prophetic acts create spiritual and natural realities. Do not despise these prophetic acts; they have great power and can do mighty things in your life.

Once you have stepped out of the Court of Records, you step into the Court of Angels. Since the Courts of Heaven complex is like an enormous building with a broad hallway. Off to each side are the various courts. It is easy for us to imagine stepping out of one court and into another down the hall. Usually, I say something like this:

> *I request permission to enter the Court of Angels this day.*

As you step in, you will often sense a lot of activity in the room. The angels are collecting papers/scrolls from others in the court. They are being dispatched to where ever they need to go. You will announce something like this:

> *I have received a ruling from the Mercy Court (or whatever court was involved), and I need angels who will carry out these orders.*

Angels will step up to receive the orders. It may be one or two angels or a large number of angels. These angels will have all kinds of appearances and be of all sizes. Some look very warlike, others very "normal". At that point, they will go forth to carry out the instructions that you received from the Court of Records.

Once completed, you will notice that even though you "gave away" the scrolls, you still have a copy with you. Take this copy and fold it into your heart. I may say:

I receive this scroll into my heart right now.

I imagine holding this scroll and pressing it to my chest. I am receiving the verdict granted by the Father in the court a short while ago. You will be able to recall what is in that paperwork at later times as you need to. You can rest assured that the Father has his angels working on your behalf.

With our operations usually complete in this court we exit the court. Remember to be thankful to our Heavenly Father for this tool given to us. We can access and enjoy the realms of Heaven.

Chapter 14
Entire QuickGuide for Ownership and Order (Personal)

Court of Titles and Deeds

I step into the realms of Heaven.

I ask permission to access the Court of Titles and Deeds and ask:

> *Are any outstanding false titles, notes or liens active against my life?*

Await the answer. Typically: a "yes" or "no."

> *What do these involve?*

Await a description, word, or picture. Often it will be only a word or two or a simple image.

The person(s) responsible created bondage in the life of the person we are representing in court. The offending party has sinned against them, and we must forgive them (John 20:23[7]). At this point we do the following:

*Your honor, we choose to forgive _____. We **forgive** them, we **bless** them[8], and we **release**[9] them from this sin and its penalties.*

If the issue was a sin committed, then:

Your honor I repent for _____ and ask your forgiveness. I ask that the blood of Jesus cover this sin now.

If you have embraced a lie or traded and it caused this lien or false title to come into play, then:

Your honor, I confess my sin of_____ and repent and ask your forgiveness. I ask that the blood of Jesus cover this sin now and ask you to release me from

---

[7] John 20:23 If you forgive the sins of any, they are forgiven them; if you retain the sins of any, they are retained.

[8] Luke 6:27-28 But I say to you who hear: Love your enemies; do good to those who hate you, [28] bless those who curse you, and pray for those who spitefully use you.

[9] Luke 4:18 The Spirit of the Lord [is] upon Me, because He has anointed Me [the Anointed One, the Messiah] to preach the good news (the Gospel) to the poor; He has sent Me to announce release to the captives and recovery of sight to the blind, to send forth as delivered those who are oppressed [who are downtrodden, bruised, crushed, and broken down by calamity]. (AMP)

its penalty. I ask that any trades involved be completely cancelled in my behalf, in Jesus' name.

Often you will sense a release. Once you feel this portion is complete, ask the following question:

Are any other false titles, notes or liens active against me?

Again, await the answer and follow the procedure in the previous paragraphs. Finally, you will ask:

Are any other false titles, notes or liens active against me?

[Typically I will limit the number of false titles, notes or liens that we are dealing with to possibly 5 or 6 at a time. We will deal with them and then return to continue the query.]

And when you get no response. At that point, make your request.

Your honor, I request that every false title be invalidated, every lien be marked satisfied, and every note be satisfied that has been against _____'s life.

As you observe the Just Judge, you may see him pouring through papers and signing or marking them in some way. He may stamp them and hand them off to a bailiff for distribution by the angels in the Court of Angels.

[In the event the Just Judge does not hand the paperwork to the bailiff, then we will step into the Court of Records and receive the paperwork, then deliver it to the Court of Angels for distribution.]

[You will often find that Holy Spirit has already hinted that He will be dealing with a particular issue by bringing it to your mind in the days immediately preceding the court session.]

You are not finished yet, however. Whenever someone (or some entity) has placed a lien, note or enacted a false title, it invariably creates situations where their life has been thrown off track. They may feel as if their life is "off-schedule." We want that corrected, and God has wonderfully provided the means to make that happen...via the Court of Times and Seasons. We will cover that procedure shortly, but first, we need to cover a variation of the steps we generally take in this court. Use the process chart when helping others in the courts.

Accessing the Court of Times and Seasons

We ask permission to enter the Court of Times and Seasons, and upon receiving permission, we step in.

You may be aware of the many clocks in the room, or of the sound of the ticking of clocks.

We announce,

We are here in regard to a readjustment of time for my life.

We ask that the timing of my life be synchronized with the timing of the Lord.

We watch and listen.

At this point, the Lord will have angels begin working on adjusting a clock relating to you or another person involved. Just observe and wait for a signal of finality – the clock clicking into place, or aligning to the 12 o'clock position, or something similar. You may hear, "It's done!"

With that complete, we now access the Court of Records (or Court of Records)

Court or Records

Upon entering the Court of Records, we make the following request:

I am requesting the records for my life for where I am right now.

[They will likely lead you to a book or box with your records. If you see a book, request permission to read the portion germane to where you are right now. If you are seeing a video or something containing a video, ask to see what you need to see for this particular time.]

Your experiences may vary from those shared in this book, but simply flow with what Holy Spirit is orchestrating for your life at this moment. When you have seen what is necessary, you will know in your knower that you are finished. Exit the Court of Records at this time.

If you have seen a video or read your book, you may also ask,

Is anything outstanding that I need to know about?

In Chapter 10 I shared about the man who had some false verdicts to deal with that was impacting his life. If you need to access the Court of Appeals, I have a process chart that will walk you through the process. It is quite simple. (Dealing with false verdicts is the focus of my book, *Overcoming Verdicts from the Courts of Hell* which is available at www.courtsofheavenbook.com.)

If the Answer is No

If the answer is no, then thank the court for allowing you access and exit the courtroom. It is then a good time to partake of Communion in remembrance of all the Lord has done for us.

If the Answer is Yes

If the answer is yes, then exit the Court of Records and request permission to access the Court of Appeals. Once at that court, present the records you received from Court of Records.

Your honor, I am here because of some outstanding false verdicts against me, and I am requesting the help of this court.

The judge will review the records and may ask you some questions. You may sense a need to repent of something and if so, follow through and repent.

He may ask what you desire specifically for the court to do for you. Make your petition and await His response. Follow any instructions given.

Once he has rendered a verdict, and you will have a sense of peace that He has done so, thank the court and exit.

If the judge handed the paperwork to an angel for dispatch, you have nothing further to do.

Court of Records & Court of Angels

If not, step into the Court of Records, request the records for the case just handled in your behalf and then take them to the Court of Angels for angelic dispatch concerning the orders within that verdict. Then receive the verdict into your heart. I often hold the verdict (the scroll) in my hand and fold it into my heart.

The following charts are available at: www.courtsofheavenbook.com.

COURT OF TIMES & SEASONS PROCESS-PERSON

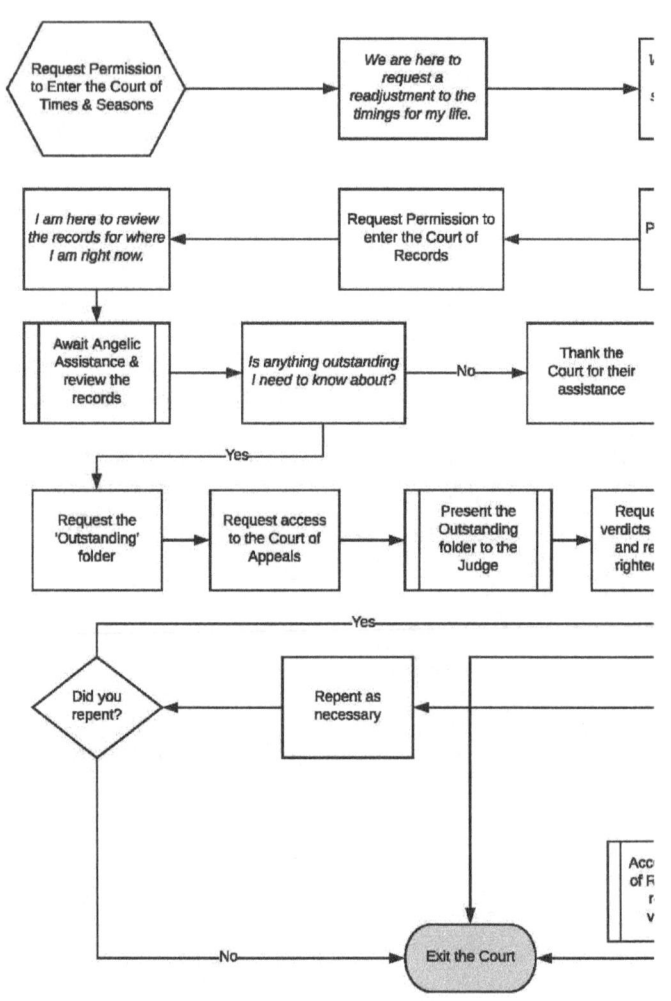

AL

Dr. Ron M. Horner | www.courtsofheavenbook.com

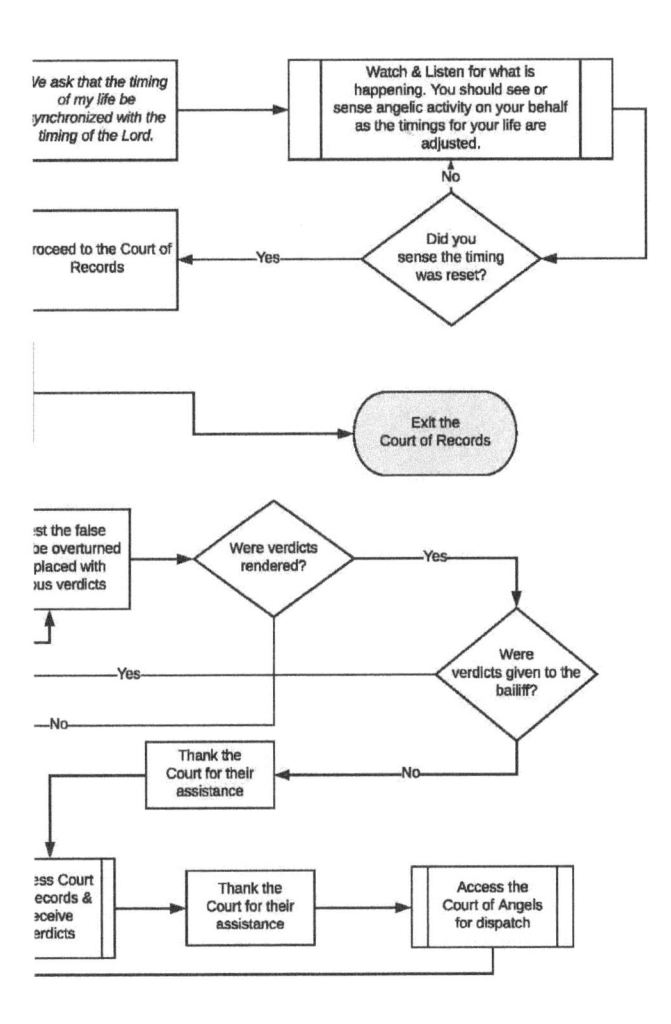

[Flowchart content:]

- We ask that the timing of my life be synchronized with the timing of the Lord.
- Watch & Listen for what is happening. You should see or sense angelic activity on your behalf as the timings for your life are adjusted.
- Did you sense the timing was reset?
  - Yes → Proceed to the Court of Records
  - No → (loop back)
- Exit the Court of Records
- Request the false [verdicts] be overturned [and] replaced with [righteous/previous] verdicts
- Were verdicts rendered?
  - Yes → Were verdicts given to the bailiff?
    - Yes → Access Court records & receive verdicts
    - No → Thank the Court for their assistance
  - No → Thank the Court for their assistance
- Thank the Court for their assistance → Access the Court of Angels for dispatch

109

Chapter 15
Entire QuickGuide
for Ownership and Order
(for Others)

If you are in a position of authority in someone's life, you have the ability to go to the courts on their behalf. If they are not under your authority (as in a child to a parent), then you usually need their express permission to pray for them. You can simply ask if you have their permission to pray for them. You don't need to tell them you are going to step into Heaven and go to court for them. They probably don't need to know that. At times the Lord will have you interceding for someone for whom you don't have specific permission or authority over. In those situations, if possible, get the cooperation of someone who does have their permission or who is in an authority situation over their life and work with them to bring forth freedom.

Court of Titles and Deeds

Step into the realms of Heaven.

We ask permission to access the Court of Titles and Deeds and ask:

> *Are any outstanding false titles, notes or liens active against _____'s life?*

Await the answer. Typically: a "yes" or "no."

> *What do these involve?*

Await a description, word, or picture. Often it will be only a word or two or a simple image.

The person(s) responsible created bondage for the person we are representing in court. The offending party has sinned against them, and we must forgive them[10]. At this point we do the following:

> *Your honor, we choose to forgive _____[*11].*
> *We **forgive** them, we **bless** them[12], and we **release**[13] them from this sin and its penalties.*

---

[10] John 20:23 If you forgive the sins of any, they are forgiven them; if you retain the sins of any, they are retained.
[11] or whoever sinned against them

If the issue was a sin committed, then:

Your honor, I confess my sin of _____ and repent and ask your forgiveness. I ask that the blood of Jesus cover this sin now and ask you to release me from its penalty. I ask that any trades involved be completely cancelled in my behalf, in Jesus' name.

If they have embraced a lie or traded and it caused this lien or false title to come into play, then:

Your honor, I repent for _____ embracing the lie that brought this situation into their life. I ask for your forgiveness and ask that this situation be remedied in their life.

Often you will sense a release. Once you feel this portion is complete, ask the following question:

Are any other false titles, notes or liens active against _____?

---

[12] Luke 6:27-28 But I say to you who hear: Love your enemies; do good to those who hate you, [28] bless those who curse you, and pray for those who spitefully use you.

[13] Luke 4:18 The Spirit of the Lord [is] upon Me, because He has anointed Me [the Anointed One, the Messiah] to preach the good news (the Gospel) to the poor; He has sent Me to announce release to the captives and recovery of sight to the blind, to send forth as delivered those who are oppressed [who are downtrodden, bruised, crushed, and broken down by calamity]. (AMP)

Again, await the answer and follow the procedure in the previous paragraphs. Finally, you will ask:

Are any other false titles, notes or liens active against _____?

[Typically I will limit the number of false titles, ntoes or liens that we are dealing with to possibly 5 or 6 at a time. We will deal with them and then return to continue the query.]

And when you get no response. At that point, make your request.

Your honor, I request that every false title by invalidated, every lien be marked satisfied, and every note be satisfied that has been that has been against _____'s life.

As you observe the Just Judge, you may see him pouring through papers and signing or marking them in some way. He may stamp them and hand them off to a bailiff for distribution by the angels in the Court of Angels.

[In the event the Just Judge does not hand the paperwork to the bailiff, then we will step into the Court of Records and receive the paperwork, then deliver it to the Court of Angels for distribution.]

[You will often find that Holy Spirit has already hinted that He will be dealing with a particular issue by bringing it to their mind in the days immediately preceding the court session.]

You are not finished yet, however. Whenever someone (or some entity) has placed a lien, note or enacted a false title, it invariably creates situations where their life has been thrown off track. They may feel as if their life is "off-schedule." We want that corrected, and God has wonderfully provided the means to make that happen...via the Court of Times and Seasons. We will cover that procedure shortly, but first, we need to cover a variation of the steps we generally take in this court. Use the process chart when helping others in the courts.

Accessing the Court of Times and Seasons

We ask permission to enter the Court of Times and Seasons, and upon receiving permission, we step in.

You may be aware of the many clocks in the room, or of the sound of the ticking of clocks.

We announce,

We are here in regard to a readjustment of time for _____.

We ask that the timing of their life be synchronized with the timing of the Lord.

We watch and listen.

At this point, the Lord will have angels begin working on adjusting a clock relating to the person involved. Just observe and wait for a signal of finality – the clock clicking into place, or aligning to the 12 o'clock position, or something similar. You may hear, "It's done!"

With that complete, we now access the Court of Records (or Court of Scribes)

Court or Records

Upon entering the Court of Records, we make the following request:

I am requesting the records for _____'s life for where they are right now.

[They will likely lead you to a book or box with their records. Do NOT be nosy. Be respectful of their records. If you see a book, request permission to read the portion germane to where they are right now. If you are seeing a video or something containing a video, ask to look at what you need to see for this particular time in their life.]

Your experiences may vary from those shared in this book, but simply flow with what Holy Spirit is orchestrating for their life at this moment. When you have seen what is necessary, you will know in your knower that you are finished. Exit the Court of Records at this time.

If you have seen a video or read their book, you may also ask,

> *Is anything outstanding that I need to know about?*

In Chapter 10 I shared about the man who had some false verdicts to deal with that was impacting his life. If you need to access the Court of Appeals, I have a process chart that will walk you through the process. It is quite simple. (Dealing with false verdicts is the focus of my book, *Overcoming Verdicts from the Courts of Hell* which is available at www.courtsofheavenbook.com.)

If the Answer is No

If the answer is no, then thank the court for allowing you access and exit the courtroom. It is then a good time to partake of Communion in remembrance of all the Lord has done for us.

If the Answer is Yes

Here is the abbreviated process for the Court of Appeals:

If the answer is yes, then exit the Court of Records and request permission to access the Court of Appeals. Once in that court, present the records you received from the Court of Records.

> *Your honor, I am here because of some outstanding false verdicts against _____ and I am requesting the help of this court.*

The judge will review the records and may ask you some questions. You may sense a need to repent of something on their behalf and if so, follow through and repent.

He may ask what you desire specifically for the court to do for them. Make your petition and await His response. Follow any instructions given.

Once he has rendered a verdict, and you will have a sense of peace that He has done so, thank the court and exit.

If the judge handed the paperwork to an angel for dispatch, you have nothing further to do.

Court of Records & Court of Angels

If not, step into the Court of Records, request the records for the case just handled in your behalf and then take them to the Court of Angels for angelic dispatch concerning the orders within that verdict.

Then receive the verdict into your heart in their behalf. I often hold the verdict (the scroll) in my hand, and simply fold it into my heart.

The following charts are available at:
www.courtsofheavenbook.com.

COURT OF TITLES & DEEDS PROCESS-OTHERS

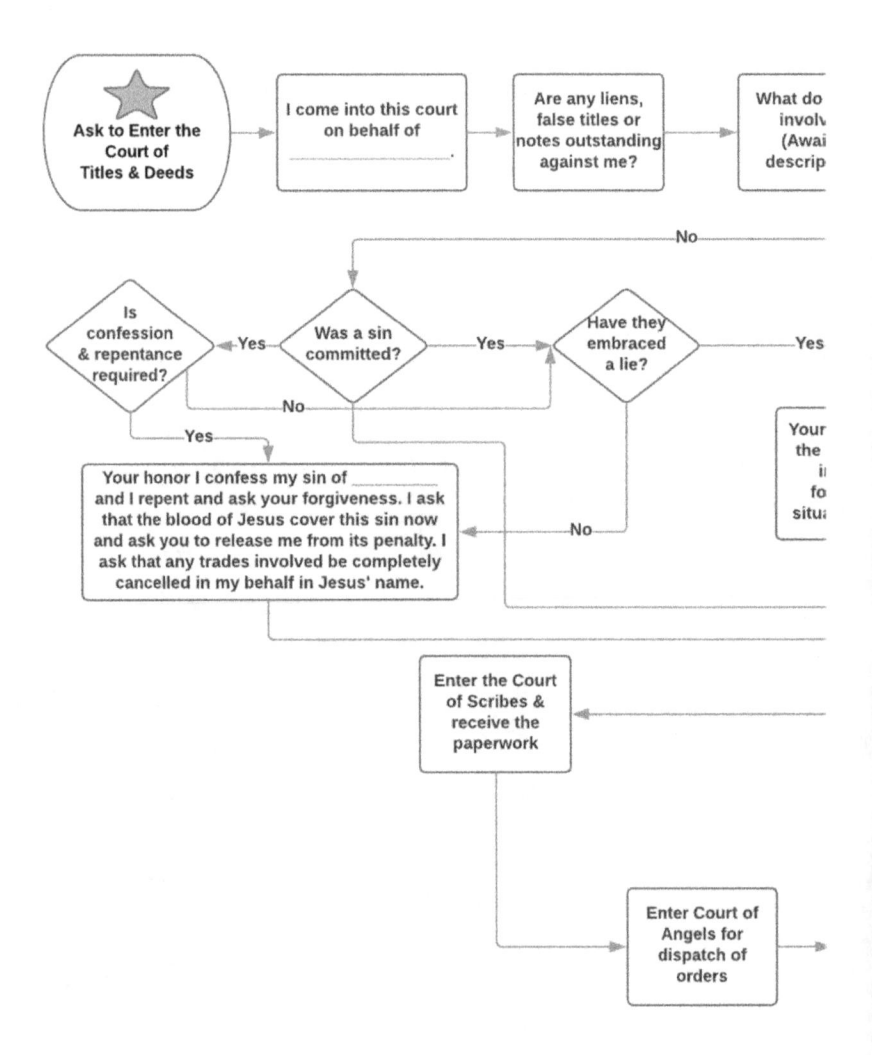

- Ask to Enter the Court of Titles & Deeds
- I come into this court on behalf of _____.
- Are any liens, false titles or notes outstanding against me?
- What do involv (Awai descrip

Is confession & repentance required? —Yes→ **Was a sin committed?** —Yes→ **Have they embraced a lie?** —Yes→ Your the i fo situa

No (from "Are any liens..." branch)

No (from "Was a sin committed?")

Yes (from "Is confession & repentance required?")

Your honor I confess my sin of _____ and I repent and ask your forgiveness. I ask that the blood of Jesus cover this sin now and ask you to release me from its penalty. I ask that any trades involved be completely cancelled in my behalf in Jesus' name.

No (from "Have they embraced a lie?")

Enter the Court of Scribes & receive the paperwork

Enter Court of Angels for dispatch of orders

Copyright ©2018 Dr. Ron M. Horner | All rights reserved (090418)

```
                                                    Dr. Ron M. Horner | www.courtsofheavenbook.com
```

```
 these                                          Your honor, we choose to forgive _____
 ve?              Is                            for their sin in this matter. We forgive them,
 it a       forgiveness      ─Yes→              we bless them and we release them from
 tion)       required?                                   this sin and its penalties.


                                                        Are any
                                                  other false titles, notes
                                                    or liens active
                                                      against me?

                                                                              No
  honor, I repent for embracing
  lie that brought this situation                             Your honor, I request that every
  into their life. I ask for your                             false title be invalidated and
  rgiveness and ask that this                                 every lien be marked 'satisfied'
  ation be remedied in their life.                            and every note be satisfied that
                                                              has been against my life.

       ──No──────────────────
                                         ──No──

                                    Did the
              ──No──           bailiff receive the     ─Yes─       Was verdict
                                    paperwork?                     rendered?


                                        Yes

    Receive the               Thank the court                    NEXT:
  → verdict into your    →      & exit         ─────→      Access the Court of
       heart                                                Times & Seasons
```

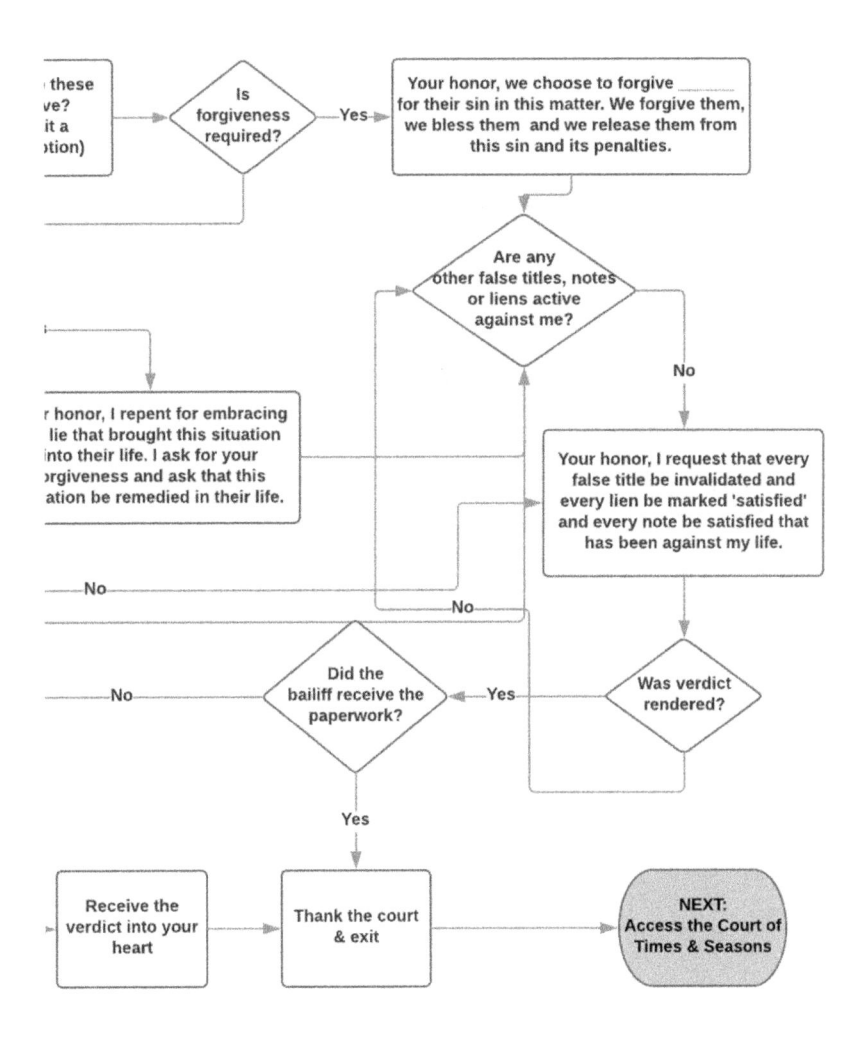

121

Chapter 16
Conclusion

The information presented in this book is ever-evolving. However, it is enough to bring great freedom into your life and into the lives of those you love. It can be a tremendous tool of intercession as it is used to free people from all sorts of bondage.

Your experiences will no doubt differ from some of the examples in this book. The wonderful thing about Heaven is the diversity and at times the humor of how God works with us. The image I saw of the angel with the hammer was almost cartoonish and as he worked he would look up and wink at me. It was quite funny to watch.

In addition so many more arenas are available for freedom. Some have had the timings of their life taken captive and it needs to be regained. Others have had their calling hijacked. That must be remedied.

I remember years ago when my grandfather was in a nursing home due to dementia. You never knew when you went to visit him what decade he would be in. However, you never let that bother you. You would simply help him do whatever he thought needed to be done at that time. On one occasion I helped him round up the cows in the pasture. (You didn't know I did some farming too, huh?) On another visit he thought the cat needed to be put outside. So, I helped him round up the cat and put it outside – the imaginary cat that is. His mind had gotten trapped in different places in time and for him this was his reality. You simply went along with it and helped him out.

Many people are like my grandfather was and are trapped in different places in time. They should have done one thing, but chose to do a different thing and as a result, everything about their life was altered. Utilizing the Court of Titles & Deeds and the Court of Times and Seasons will enable us to get back on track. Own the sin that got you into the mess you found yourself in. Repent and ask the blood of Jesus to be applied. Let freedom come. He is the redeemer of lost time in our lives and his grace and power is so thorough that he can make our situations as if they never occurred at all. This applies not only to us, but to our families, cities, states, and even nations.

As these principles are applied entire groups of people can be freed. For anything we wish to happen in the natural, it must first be handled in the realm of the spirit. The possibilities are endless. May the Lord enhance our understanding of these courts and others to bring freedom and life to many.

Bibliography

American Standard Version. Unknown, 1901.

Amplified® Bible. The Lockman Foundation, 1987.

Crossway. ESV® Bible (The Holy Bible, English Standard Version®). Nashville: Good News Publishers, 2001.

Foundation, The Lockman. The Amplified Bible. Grand Rapids: Zondervan, 1958.

"New Testament." Simmons, Brian. The Passion Translation. BroadStreet Publishing, 2017.

Thomas Nelson. New King James Version. Nashville: Thomas Nelson Publishers, 1982.

Description

Have you ever felt as if your life was not really in control? Have you felt your life was out of sync with where God really wanted you to be? We have found the culprit! We have an enemy who tries to usurp ownership over our lives and does so in insidious ways. He creates false title deeds, notes and liens against us that hinder and keep us from the forward progress we need.

In this book, you will find the simple solution for coming into freedom. You will learn how to access the Court of Titles & Deeds, the Court of Times and Seasons, as well as the Court of Records. You will find freedom and know how to bring it to others.

The results are powerful. Don't wait another day! Step in today!

About the Author

Dr. Ron Horner is an apostolic teacher specializing in *Engaging the Courts of Heaven, Overcoming Verdicts from the Courts of Hell, Overturning the False Verdicts of Freemasonry* and other bondages, and the subject of this book – *Engaging the Courts of Heaven*. He is married and the father of three daughters (two of whom are married), and grandfather to Ike and Levi. He resides in central North Carolina with his wife, Adina and youngest daughter, Darian. He is the author of four books on the Courts of Heaven prayer paradigm.

Contact us to conduct seminars on the Courts of Heaven to your church, ministry, or group.

www.courtsofheavenbook.com

Recommended Resources

Engaging the Mercy Court of Heaven

(formerly *The Courts of Heaven: An Introduction*)
Embracing a New Paradigm of Prayer

by Dr. Ron M. Horner
Paperback: $19.99
Spiral Edition: $24.99
Kindle Edition: $9.99
PDF Edition: $19.99

In Luke 18 Jesus subtly introduces a third paradigm of prayer. The courtroom paradigm has gone overlooked throughout church history. Only in the last few years has this truth been uncovered with amazing results. Prayers that have long gone unanswered are being answered in a matter of days or even hours. Situations which seemed hopeless are turning around.

This truth is for every believer, but it will also help thrust efforts of intercession into new levels of a breakthrough. Once every legal obstacle hindering the answer to your prayers is removed, the answers will come. As we learn to engage the Courts of Heaven, lives will change. Your life will change. You will experience answered prayer on a level you may not have thought possible.

Grasp these truths and begin to engage the Courts of Heaven. The court is now in session…all rise!

Also available in Spanish.

Available at www.courtsofheavenbook.com

Engaging the Courts of Heaven

Maximizing the Power of the Courts

by Dr. Ron M. Horner
Paperback: $19.99
Spiral Edition: $24.99
Kindle Edition: $9.99
PDF Edition: $19.99

Available for every believer is access to the Court System of Heaven. This book will introduce you to several of these courts, and their purpose, function, and jurisdiction. Adding the knowledge of these courts will empower you in your intercession for your family, church, and the nations of the earth.

Whether dealing with land issues, church or ministry issues, or situations with your business, the answers to your questions lie within the pages of this book – *Engaging the Courts of Heaven*. Engage, access, and see the power of the Court System of Heaven!

Available at www.courtsofheavenbook.com

Engaging the Help Desk of the Courts of Heaven

Come boldly! Come often!

by Dr. Ron M. Horner
Paperback: $9.99
Kindle Edition: $5.99
PDF Edition: $9.99

In order to help us learn the Court System of Heaven, the Just Judge has provided a straightforward means of aiding us – a Help Desk. As we are learning to maneuver in the courts, we can just step up to the help desk and describe the issue to the attendant. Then ask, "Where should I go to deal with this?"

This straightforward approach will help us learn to navigate the intricacies of the Courts of Heaven. Find out the myriad ways help is available to us. Help is waiting. Come on in!

Available at www.courtsofheavenbook.com

Overcoming Verdicts from the Courts of Hell

Releasing False Judgements

by Dr. Ron M. Horner
Paperback: $14.99
Kindle Edition: $7.99
PDF Edition: $ 14.99

    Have you found yourself struggling with situations or mindsets from which you could find no relief? We have not yet awakened to the fact that we may have been facing a false judgment arising out of the Courts of Hell. Jesus promised us in Matthew 16:18 that the Gates of Hell would not prevail against the church, but that promise was predicated on our using the keys effectively – the keys of binding and loosing! This is not your typical "binding and loosing" book. It explores a whole different dimension and unveils what you are dealing with and how to successfully overcome these false judgments affecting your lives. You need this book NOW!

Available at www.courtsofheavenbook.com

Overturning the False Verdicts of Freemasonry

Freedom from Scottish Rite & York Rite Freemasonry

by Dr. Ron M. Horner
Paperback: $19.99
Spiral Bound: $24.99
Kindle Edition: $9.99
PDF Edition: $19.99

Few organizations in human history have integrated themselves at every level of society like Freemasonry. Men (and women in specific sectors) take oaths to demon gods that bind them, their families, and their future generations to covenants and verdicts that bring destruction on their entire bloodlines. The insidious nature of these organizations [-- the Scottish Rite, the York Rite, Shriners and their many offshoots and entanglements (including the Illuminati) were borne in the councils of Hell.] This book will help unveil the false verdicts that empower the resulting curses that, on every level of one's life, bring ultimate destruction or fear of destruction. The oaths have bound once honest men to dishonesty, treachery and even murder. Outsiders, who look at the various oaths and entanglements often wonder what would make men take vows such as those required by Freemasonry. Why would otherwise sensible men do such things?

Available at www.courtsofheavenbook.com

Divorced!

Obtaining Freedom from the Sun and Moon god

by Jeanette Strauss & Doug Carr
Edited by Dr. Ron M. Horner
Paperback: $14.99
Spiral Bound: $19.99
Kindle Edition: $7.99
PDF Edition: $ 19.99

The Body of Christ has been facing an enemy that it has little knowledge or understanding of. Much less has the Body known how to overcome this insidious foe – the principality of Baal, the sun god, and his counterpart Allah, the moon god. We must divorce these principalities from our lives in order to make the necessary progress in our daily lives.

The strategy to gain the victory over these principalities is through Courts of Heaven intercession. We will obtain the legal right through repentance and forgiveness for sin committed against God to remove the lawful rights Baal and Allah has used to withhold from us and our families, churches, businesses, cities, towns, and regions. This series of petitions of divorce are geared for individual, family, church or ministry, businesses, or regions or territories. Utilize these petitions to gain the freedom purchased by the blood of Jesus Christ.

Available at www.courtsofheavenbook.com

Silencing the Accuser

Restoration of Your Spiritual Birthright
(Third Edition)

by Jacquelin & Daniel Hanselman
Paperback: $19.99
Spiral Bound: $24.99
Kindle Edition: $9.99
PDF Edition: $ 19.99

The Body of Christ is being destroyed by lack of knowledge, wisdom, and understanding of the captivity of individuals, families, cities, and even nations caused by generational and personal accusations. The reality of the goodness of God is challenged by the stark contrast between the covenantal blessings promised in the Word of God and the struggles in one's life.

In this book, the Hanselmans uncover the source of these hindrances with practical teachings and prayers that will help you be cleared of the charges against you and your family in the Courts of Heaven. Allow the Just Judge to declare you innocent by the Blood of the Lamb as you agree with your accuser in generational and personal repentance. Now is the time to begin the process of dismantling the accusations of the enemy! Families, regions, and nations can be set free by the application of these prayers. It is time for the destiny of the Body of Christ to be released for the great end-time harvest.

Available at www.silencingtheaccuser.com